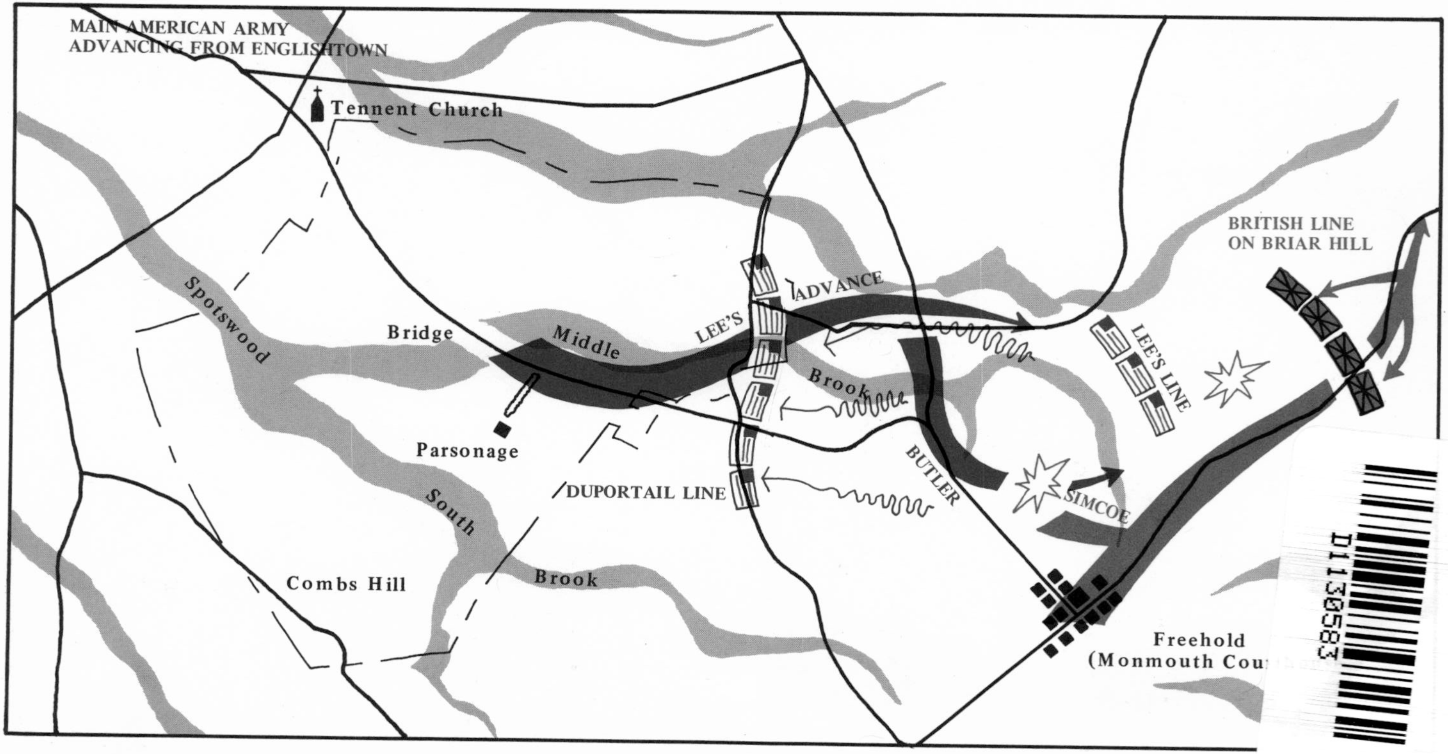

D1130583

BRITISH LINE
ON BRIAR HILL

LEE'S LINE

SIMCOE

Freehold
(Monmouth Cou

ADVANCE

LEE'S

Brook

BUTLER

Middle

DUPORTAIL LINE

Parsonage

South

Brook

Combs Hill

Bridge

Spotswood

Tennent Church

MAIN AMERICAN ARMY
ADVANCING FROM ENGLISHTOWN

Map No. 2

Lee's Advance to Briar Hill and Retreat to the Duportail Line

THE MAKING OF A SCAPEGOAT

By Theodore Thayer

Israel Pemberton, King of the Quakers
1943

Pennsylvania Politics and the Growth of Democracy, 1740–1776
1953

Nathanael Greene: Strategist of the American Revolution
1960

The Story of Old Elizabethtown
1964

Yorktown: Campaign of Strategic Options
1975

Colonial and Revolutionary Morris County, New Jersey
1975

The Making of a Scapegoat: Washington and Lee at Monmouth
1976

Kennikat Press
National University Publications
Series in American Studies

General Editor
James P. Shenton
Professor of History, Columbia University

Charles Lee. Esq.
Major General of the American Forces

THEODORE THAYER

THE MAKING OF A SCAPEGOAT

Washington and Lee at Monmouth

National University Publications
KENNIKAT PRESS // 1976
Port Washington, N. Y. // London

Manufactured in the United States of America

Published by
Kennikat Press Corp.
Port Washington, N.Y./London

Library of Congress Cataloging in Publication Data

Thayer, Theodore George, 1904–
     The making of a scapegoat.

     (Series in American studies) (Kennikat Press
national university publications)
     Bibliography: p.
     Includes index.
     1. Lee, Charles, 1731–1782. 2. Monmouth,
Battle of, 1778. I. Title.
E207.L47T46   973.3'34'0924 [B]   76-7477
ISBN 0-8046-9139-8

Contents

Preface

Since the War of Independence numerous historians have written of the great victory Washington would have won at Monmouth had General Charles Lee obeyed orders and attacked the British with his formidable advanced corps. Because he did not attack, Lee has been unmercifully condemned as a blackguard and a traitor who, out of jealousy, desired to have Washington fail. Some historians go so far as to see in his actions a traitorous plan to aid the enemy by disobeying orders.

A close examination of what happened on this momentous day provides a much different interpretation. As we follow the moves of the armies and study the evidence, it becomes clear that had Lee stood his ground the Americans very likely would have suffered a catastrophic defeat. Washington's main army, miles away, could not have prevented Lee's corps from being cut to pieces by Sir Henry Clinton's regulars. Should this have been accomplished, Washington's whole army would have been in danger of being surrounded and forced to surrender. It is possible, therefore, that the Battle of Monmouth would have brought the Revolution to an inglorious close at the very time when the prospect of victory with the aid of France seemed most promising.

Lee, moreover, accomplished more than the saving of the American army from defeat. Having led the British into a pocket formed by Washington's main force, he gave his commander in chief an opportunity to entrap and destroy the flower of the British army by a flanking movement. By not doing so, Washington, it would seem, lost a golden opportunity to end the war with a great American victory.

After the battle some men in Congress declared that Lee had saved the day at Monmouth. The country, however, would not back him for fear of offending Washington, who had severely upbraided Lee on the battlefield for his retreat. In bitterness, Lee made the fatal error of criticizing Washington and lost the support of many sympathizers. The rancor arising from the issue has beclouded the Battle of Monmouth to this day. Now, after nearly two hundred years, it is hoped that Charles Lee can at last be considered objectively and given the credit due him.

For reading the manuscript and offering welcome suggestions, I am indebted to Professor Russell F. Weigley. I also wish to thank Mr. Donald Sinclair, Curator of Special Collections, Rutgers University, as well as Dr. Francis S. Ronalds, Mr. Melvin Weig, and Mr. Steven H. Lewis, successively superintendents of Morristown National Historical Park. Likewise, I am indebted to Bruce Stewart, Historian at the Morristown National Historical Park, Mr. Robert M. Lunny and his staff at the New Jersey Historical Society, Mr. Kenneth Richards of the State Library at Trenton, and Mr. Gilbert Cohen, Mr. James Doele, Mr. Morris Sherman, and Mr. James K. Merritt at the Dana Library of Rutgers University, who have all rendered their assistance. The maps were made by Edwards and Kelsey, Newark, under the direction of Mr. Kenneth Creveling, Jr. Permission to use them was given by Mr. Joseph J. Truncer, Director of the Division of Parks and Forests at Trenton, New Jersey. For typing and copyreading, I thank Maryanne Thayer.

THE MAKING OF A SCAPEGOAT

Liberty to be endurable
ought to be on the broadest base possible.
                                        Charles Lee

Time and posterity
will do you [Charles Lee] justice.
                                        Benjamin Rush

GENERAL CHARLES LEE
(From the Print Division of the New York Public Library)

I

Washington and Lee

General John Burgoyne's surrender of his British army at Saratoga in October 1777 to General Horatio Gates was hailed as a victory which would lead to a speedy termination of the War of Independence. Everywhere in America General Gates was toasted as a great military genius who had brought about the surprising turn of events.

In contrast to Gates, Washington had won no crippling victories over the enemy. Rather, except for the life-saving victories at Trenton and Princeton he had met with nothing but defeat at the hands of his skillful antagonist, Sir William Howe. It is not strange, therefore, that after Gates's victory at Saratoga Washington found himself the target for critics who questioned his generalship and pointed to his repeated failure on the field of battle.

The galling thought of his misfortunes while his subordinate was winning the laurels of a conquering hero must have borne heavily on Washington. His yearning for a great victory—one that would humiliate the enemy and disarm his critics—must have amounted to an obsession as his failures multiplied. It was therefore perhaps from a feeling of frustration that he finally erupted at Monmouth. There, on the field of battle, in a towering rage Washington reprimanded General Charles Lee for retreating and losing, as was thought, an opportunity for winning a momentous victory.

This dramatic meeting of Washington and Lee ended in the disgrace of Charles Lee and his dismissal from the American army. Eventually it led to General Lee's being labeled by historians as a traitor and a man devoid of principles. This belief has become so ingrained in American history that to present General Lee as a scapegoat for Washington's failures at Monmouth requires an impartial approach and a thorough reexamination of a fascinating chapter of American history.

The defeats which haunted Washington had begun when General William Howe, as commander in chief of the British army in America, first appeared at New York, in 1776, with a firm determination to crush the rebellion with one grand stroke and thus bring the conflict to a close with as little bloodshed as possible. Had Howe pushed a little harder (and had he had a little more luck), his objectives might well have been realized before winter began.

In the first major battle of this campaign, Washington was outgeneraled and outfought on Long Island, where Howe cut to ribbons the American advanced corps under Major General John Sullivan. A few weeks later, at Harlem Heights and White Plains, Washington's army showed some promise in that it gave a minor setback to the enemy, even though it was eventually forced to retreat. This was followed by the stunning surrender of nearly three thousand Americans as the British forced the surrender of Fort Washington. Thereafter, Washington's escape through New Jersey to the protection of the Pennsylvania side of the Delaware gave all the appearance of a military disaster; his seemed to be a defeated army on the verge of disbanding. Apparently only victory by a surprise attack on the Hessians at Trenton on a cold December morning saved the Continental army for dissolution.

During 1777, while the Northern army was winnng laurels with General Gates, Washington suffered more defeats. Routed in a hardfought battle at Brandywine, the Americans were pushed aside, and Howe marched triumphantly into Philadelphia. Defeat again befell Washington when he vainly attempted to oust the British from Philadelphia by a surprise attack on their lines at Germantown. Some sharp fighting for the control of the Delaware ended again with victory for the British. Thus closed a campaign which, although it ended unfortunately for Washington, made it possible for Gates to force the surrender of Burgoyne while Howe was far away in Pennsylvania.

Soon after the enemy secured control of the Delaware River, Washington brought his tired and ragged troops to Valley Forge. Meanwhile his trusted lieutenant, Major General Nathanael Greene, sought to convince people that the commander in chief had performed miracles in the face of an enemy of superior strength. His efforts, however, met with but partial success. Already critics were comparing Washington unfavorably to Gates, in whose hands the salvation of the country seemed to rest.[1]

Criticism of Washington surfaced following the exposure of a letter written by Major General Thomas Conway to General Gates. According to the report Conway had written "Heaven has determined to save your Country, or a weak General and Bad Councellors would have ruined it." Years later, Alexander Graydon declared that he had heard Conway say that although Washington was a true gentleman, he had no talent as a general.[2]

Upon learning of Conway's letter to Gates by a note from Major General Lord Stirling, Washington sent the message to Conway without elaboration. The latter denied that he had written any such opinions, but few believed him. Henry Laurens, in fact, declared that in reality Conway's censure of Washington was even more derogatory than reported.

Conway's censure of Washington was universally condemned throughout the Continental army, where esteem for the commander in chief remained high. Conway, moreover, was disliked by most of his fellow officers. A veteran of foreign wars and a former colonel in the French army, Conway was an aggressive young man who irritated most of his companions in arms. Although he had exhibited considerable bravery at Brandywine and Germantown, officers like Nathanael Green were not impressed with his ability. Furthermore, they especially disliked his constant angling for recognition and promotion.

Although the army remained solidly behind Washington, within the walls of Congress things were different. Soon it was rumored that many delegates wanted to have Washington replaced by General Gates. This so-called Conway Cabal has attracted the attention of historians from that day to this. Nineteenth-century historians in general were inclined to believe that there was an actual conspiracy to bring about Washington's removal. Twentieth-century historians, however, have concluded that although Washington suffered from criticism, there was never any cabal intent upon removing him. Indeed, when Washington came under fire he found that he had an amazing amount of support both in Congress and in the country at large.

Adding fuel to the fire, Congress promoted Conway to the position of inspector general of the army with the rank of major general. Greene blamed Gates for recommending the promotion, which touched off a wave of discontent in the army. Nine brigadiers, who had been passed over in favor of Conway, sent a memorial to Congress protesting the promotion. One of the intriguers who supported Conway and criticized Washington, in Greene's opinion, was Thomas Mifflin, erstwhile quartermaster general and an important political figure in Pennsylvania. All three—Gates, Conway, and Mifflin—were motivated, Greene thought, by "great ambition" and would sacrifice "everything for their private views." Greene soon noted that neither Lafayette nor the other French officers would speak to Conway, who found the official atmosphere as cold as the surrounding air.[3]

In Congress the foremost critics of Washington were Richard Henry Lee, James Lovell, Benjamin Rush, Thomas Burke, and John and Samuel Adams. Richard Henry Lee, one of the principal leaders of the independence movement in Virginia, was considered by many to be a leading opponent of Washington. Lee, whose views generally coincided with those of John and Samuel Adams, usually allied himself with the Massachusetts delegates. After the Battle of Monmouth, Richard Henry Lee and the Adamses took General Lee's side in the great dispute over the retreat during the battle. Benjamin Harrison, another Virginian and a friend of Washington, revealed what congressmen were thinking when he wrote:

We have a story circulating here that there has been a motion made in Congress to divide the command of the army and that RHL was at the bottom of it. . . . We are also informed that Gen. Washington's character has been attacked publicly by S. & J. Adams. . . .[4]

Soon the Virginia-New England coalition succeeded in placing General Gates at the head of the newly created Board of War, a move which many considered a strategy to discredit Washington. The junto also set about arranging an expedition against Canada, under Conway's command. This effort, however, raised such a storm of opposition in Congress and in the army that Lafayette was then appointed the commander of the expedition. It never materialized. Although John and Samuel Adams had taken a prominent part in making Washington commander in chief in 1775, they never hesitated to criticize him when they thought occasion warranted. Before the Conway affair, John Adams spoke out in favor of more congressional control over the appointment and promotion of officers, so that less heed would be taken of what Washington and his staff recommended. Congress, he said, was too prone "to idolize an image which their own hands have molded. . . I speak here of the superstitious veneration that is sometimes paid to General Washington."[5]

Though Adams habitually criticized, he, for one, did not at any time actually favor Washington's removal. Henry Knox reported that John Adams told him, at the time of the Conway incident, that he considered Washington "the center of our Union." Samuel Adams was apparently of the same opinion. Years later, in a letter to Richard Henry Lee, he wrote: "I have always had a very high esteem for the late Commander-in-Chief of our Armies."[6]

James Lovell, another delegate to Congress from Massachusetts, was more extreme in his attacks on Washington than the Adamses. As a young schoolmaster, he had delivered the oration at the first anniversary of the Boston Massacre. Four years later, he was arrested for spying and was held a prisoner in a Halifax jail until his father succeeded in getting him exchanged. He returned to Massachusetts in broken health, but remained no less determined to carry on in the struggle for independence.

Elected to Congress, Lovell became secretary for foreign affairs, in which office his fluency in French proved serviceable in winning the aid of France. After Washington's defeats at Brandywine and Germantown, he was outspoken in his criticism of the commander in chief. Writing to Gates, he said:

We have had a noble Army melted down by ill-judged marches, marches that disgrace their authors and Directors & which have occasioned the Severest & most just Sarcasm & Contempt of our Enemies. How much are you to be envied, my dear General? How different your Conduct & your Fortune! In short, this Army will be totally lost unless you come down & collect the virtuous Band, who wish to fight under your Banner, & with their aid save the Southern Hemisphere.[7]

Hardly less critical of Washington was Benjamin Rush, the Philadelphia physician who had recently resigned as surgeon general of the medical corps of the Continental army. All of these men, it should be remembered, would prove to be sympathetic to General Lee after the dramatic confrontation at Monmouth. "Look at both [Washington and Gates]," cried Rush after Burgoyne's surrender, "the one on the pinnacle of military glory—the other out-generaled and twice beaten."[8] Another critic, Thomas Burke, a delegate from North Carolina and later a war governor of the state, thought that although Washington was a towering patriot, he was not essential for the salvation of the country. No man, he declared, was indispensable.[9]

Washington was not insensitive to the attacks of his critics. He wrote to Patrick Henry:

My caution to avoid anything, that could injure the service, prevented me from communicating, but to a very few of my friends, the intrigues of a faction, which I know was formed against me, since it might serve to publish out internal dissentions; but their own restless Zeal to advance their views has too clearly betrayed them, and made concealment, on my part, fruitless. I cannot precisely mark the extent to their views, but it appeared in general, that General Gates was to be exalted, on the ruin of my reputation and influence. . . . General Mifflin, it is commonly supposed, bore the second part in the Cabal; and General Conway, I know, was a very active and malignant Partisan. . . . [10]

Although criticism of Washington ran high in governmental circles, the opposition soon found itself floundering in a tidal wave of support for Washington. "I am glad," wrote George Lux, a member of Congress from Maryland, "that the faction & designing Junto who would sacrifice everything to their insatiable Ambition, are alarmed at their unpopularity on account of their malevolent machinations, & now deny all their Practices."[11] So sweeping was the change of sentiment in Congress that Richard Peters, in January, was convinced that if an election were held the commander in chief would be unanimously reappointed.[12]

Indeed, the outcry against the critics of Washington grew so loud that these same critics were driven to console themselves with the thought that they were martyrs to the cause of free speech. A few months later, when General Lee felt the sting of public opinion, he likewise lamented that no one dared to criticize Washington and expect to escape public reprobation. In the aftermath, General Gates affirmed that he had never conspired to obtain the supreme command. "For my part," he wrote, "I solemnly declare, I never was engaged in any plan or plot for the removal of General Washington, nor do I believe any such ever existed."[13]

Conway did resign from the Continental army; but before he retired he was wounded in a duel with General Cadwalader, who had accused him of cowardice at Germantown. Conway, believing he was dying, affirmed that he never intended any harm to Washington, whom he looked upon as a good and true man.[14]

While the British were in Philadelphia, Washington presented Sir William Howe with an opportunity to deal the American army a crippling blow. On May 18, 1778, the Marquis de Lafayette marched from Valley Forge with twenty-five hundred of Washington's best troops. The force took five cannon for what was hoped to be a surprise attack on the enemy's outer defenses surrounding Philadelphia. It was a dangerous, if not foolhardy, undertaking because the Schuylkill River separated Lafayette's corps from Washington's main army at Valley Forge. As has been said, the force with Lafayette was too small for a major engagement and too large for a raiding party.

But the twenty-year-old Lafayette, who had captivated Washington, succeeded in persuading the commander in chief to make the commitment.[15] To entrust so large and important a segment of the army to a youth with no military experience still seems an incredible act.

Lafayette was barely over the Schuylkill before swift-riding Loyalists alerted Howe of the move. Sir William was elated. At once he ordered General James Grant to take a strong force of five thousand and march to the rear of Lafayette's corps near Barron Hill to the north of the city. Another two thousand under General Charles Grey advanced by the Ridge Road. Howe was so certain that Lafayette would be encircled and taken that he sent out invitations for a dinner with the marquis.[16]

Fortunately for Lafayette, his band of scouts captured two wandering grenadiers near Three Mile Run and learned what was happening. Word reached him about daybreak. But by the time he had found a route of escape over a nearby ford, Grant was closing in on the seemingly trapped Americans. Before launching his attack, however, he waited for word from Grey and rested his division after a twenty-mile march. This gave Lafayette's men an opportunity of running for their lives; a few stayed behind to mislead the enemy. As the men plunged into a river swollen by heavy rains, they locked arms to prevent being swept away by the current. Some men drowned and others lost their muskets. Before the last of the Americans gained the opposite bank, the British appeared at the river's edge. No escape could have been a closer one. Because the corps made its escape, Washington did not receive much criticism, but there were some who spoke of the folly of the undertaking.[17]

In April 1778, while Washington and the Continental army were at Valley Forge, General Charles Lee was exchanged for General Richard Prescott. He had been a prisoner at New York ever since his capture in December 1776, during the retreat through New Jersey. For the first six months of his captivity, he had been held a prisoner on the *Centurion,* on which at times he had reason to complain of the treatment he received.

After his captivity, General Lee soon found that Sir William Howe had virtually no sympathy for him. He was, said Howe, nothing more than an outright traitor who deserved to be hanged. Consequently, Howe ordered his adjutant general to prosecute Lee for desertion from the British army. Action, however, was dropped when it was reported that Lee had resigned his commission in a letter to Viscount Barrington written just before he joined the American army. A few months later his name was stricken from half pay by the authorities in London. Congress then resolved to indemnify Lee for any losses in property he might suffer through confiscation by the British.[18]

Frustrated but not yet willing to drop charges against Lee, Howe wrote to Germain, the secretary of war, for clarification of the case. Upon learning that Lee was in danger, Congress moved to protect him by declaring that he had no connection with the British army when he volunteered to fight for America. If any harm came to him, Congress warned, it would retaliate. Though this action ended Howe's attempt to prosecute Lee, he stubbornly refused to include him in the exchange of prisoners, partly out of malice and partly, it would seem, from his high regard for Lee's ability and his desire to prevent Washington from gaining the benefit of his talent.[19]

The treatment accorded Lee eased after Howe received orders from London to consider him as a prisoner of war. General Henry Clinton also interceded and had Lee transferred to New York. Here with two old cronies of the Forty-Fourth Regiment he took up quarters above the council chamber. Permitted all the comforts of life as well as the freedom of the city, after Burgoyne's surrender, Lee found that his life as a captive was not so bad. Each night, after consuming a quantity of good wine, he tumbled into bed with little to trouble his mind. To be sure, he never lacked company, for he was generally admired as a clever conversationalist "with a shrewd affection of great knowledge of the world and of high society." He was especially friendly with General James Robertson, the commandant of New York, as well as with Clinton and any number of other officers. Only Howe avoided him.[20]

A lover of English traditions, Lee seems always to have entertained the thought that reconciliation between America and Great Britain was desirable. As early as the Boston campaign when the British took Bunker Hill at such a frightful cost, Lee corresponded with Burgoyne and Cornwallis in a continuing debate over the issues which had caused the war. A staunch Whig, he defended traditional English liberties against a king and his sycophants, who were determined to govern the empire with a despotic hand.

After his imprisonment, Lee still hoped that reconciliation would bring an end to the civil war. With this in mind, in March 1777, he wrote to Congress asking that two or three representatives be sent to New York to talk with the Howes. Hearing this, the Reverend William Gordon, the historian of the Revolution, wrote suspiciously, "What has Lee been after of late? Suffering himself to be made a pawn of by the Howes."[21]

No reply came from Congress; it rightfully feared the adverse effect such a move would have on France. However, Greene, who normally opposed such measures, thought it might do no harm to send more delegates to New York. John Adams disagreed. In a letter he held that "it appears to be an artful strategem of the two grateful brothers to hold up to the public view the phantom of a negotiation, in order to give spirit and courage to the Tories, to distract and divide the Whigs at a critical moment, when the utmost exertions are necessary to draw together an army."[22]

The refusal of Congress to send men to New York was a decided embarrassment to Lee, who apparently saw himself in the role of a skillful diplomat who would restore the empire to its former glory. "It is a most unfortunate circumstance for myself," he wrote Washington, "and I think no less so for the public, that the Congress have not thought proper to comply with my request. It could not possible have been attended with any ill consequences, and might with good ones. At least it was an indulgence, which I thought my situation entitled me to. . . ."[23]

Just ten days after Lee requested Congress to send a delegation to New York, he formulated a plan by which he thought Howe could end the war and thus terminate a struggle which was draining both countries of their resources in men and wealth. In a paper, he professed his belief that the Howes wanted to see an end to the war as much as he did. His plan for subduing the colonies was simple. The Howes should cut off the South by taking Annapolis, Alexandria, and Baltimore, thus depriving the North of Southern help. He reasoned that in less than two months the rebellion would crumble and collapse if the Howes followed his plan.

Whether the Howes gave Lee's proposal any consideration is not known. Dated March 29, 1777, the paper was endorsed by Sir William's secretary and filed as "Plan of Mr. Lee, 1777." The plan in itself was far from novel, and it could only have made Howe aware that a man of Lee's ability recommended such a course. George Moore, who discovered the paper eighty years later, thought that it prompted Howe to desert Burgoyne and move against Philadelphia. Other historians have pointed out that if it had any bearing on Howe's going south instead of staying to help Burgoyne, it rendered America a great service. Troyer S. Anderson, an authority on the Howe brothers, thought that it had no bearing on their decision.[24]

Naturally there has been much speculation as to why Lee indulged in this traitorous or at least compromising suggestion. No doubt he did it partly to flatter his ego by ingratiating himself with the Howes. Nevertheless, on a deeper level, it was doubtlessly inspired by his belief that if possible the empire should be reunited. Admittedly, given his ideas and inclinations, the resumption of his command in the Continental army makes suspect all his subsequent actions.

Of about the age of Washington, Lee was the youngest son of General John Lee and his wife Isabella, a daughter of Sir Henry Bunbury. He was born in 1731, and by the time his father died in 1750, he had acquired a classical education both at the King Edward VI free school at Bury Saint Edmunds and at an academy in Switzerland. He liked Shakespeare, studied history, and, as a child of the Enlightenment, immersed himself in the writings of Rousseau and Voltaire. During his army career on the Continent, he learned to speak French fluently and had a knowledge of Polish, German, Italian, and Spanish.

In 1751, Lee received a lieutenant's commission in his deceased father's regiment, the Forty-Fourth Irish Establishment, commanded by Thomas Gage. Three years later he went to America with General Braddock. Some accounts report his performing valiantly at Braddock's Field, where he was one of the last to quit the ground.

Although a man of average height, Lee was conspicuous by his extremely thin frame and his long, acquiline nose. At one time during the Revolution, when he asked a man with a big nose why he kept turning his head aside while talking with him, the man answered that he was afraid their noses might collide. Lee laughed and gave the man a dollar for his wit. At another time, a servant girl took him with his slovenly dress to be a common soldier and commanded him to help her in the kitchen. He complied. During the work, the girl told him how she hoped to see General Lee who, she heard, was the oddest and ugliest man in the army. Lee afterwards told the story to an aide-de-camp; it proved, he said, that clothes make the man, for "neither virtue nor abilities without it, will make you look like a gentleman."[25]

Washington Irving observed that Lee was ingenuous by nature and not given to intrigue.[26] However, he could be as cutting as a knife and devastatingly sarcastic to those who offended him. Naturally, his wit and humor gained him a large following. Count Lippe-Bückeburg commander in chief of the allied forces in Portugal, declared that Lee was "a sublime genius, highly improved by books and travel. . . ." He was "eccentric, but with asperity of tongue, impudent, from a disposition to guard himself from cramping independence."[27]

With the exception of his Indian wife, Lee never was a success with the ladies: he was too homely, and his unconventional manners were distasteful to them. Yet he was always respectful of their interests. To Lady Blake he confided that he long lamented "the accursed prevailing notion that women ought to have defective educations."[28]

Although knowledgeable and accomplished, Lee could be moody and irascible, traits which in the end spelled his ruin. Deeming himself superior to most men, he disliked taking orders from anyone and was usually contemptuous of his commanding officers. Generally, however, his faultfinding was not simply a matter of personal spite. In the case of Braddock, Lee contrarily rose to that general's defense after his calamitous defeat.

Lee served with distinction throughout the French and Indian War.

At Ticonderoga, while serving under General James Abercromby, he sustained a serious wound and was taken to Albany, where Mrs. Philip Schuyler nursed him back to health. He was greatly moved by her generosity. "He swore, in his vehement manner, that he was sure there would be a place reserved for Madame in heaven, though no other woman should be there, and that he should wish nothing better than to share her final destiny."[29]

Lee nearly met his death in the Niagara campaign in 1759. Two bullets creased his hair during the siege of the fort. Then, while he was among the Iroquois, he married a Seneca girl. "My wife," he wrote to his beloved sister, Sidney Lee, "is the daughter of the famous White Thunder who is Belt of Wampum to the Senecas which is in fact their Lord Treasurer. She is a very great beauty and is more like your friend Mrs. Griffith than anybody I know. I shall say nothing of her accomplishments for you must be certain that a Woman of her fashion cannot be without many."[30]

By this time he had been adopted by the Indians and given the name Ounewaterika, signifying boiling water or "one whose spirits are never asleep."[31] After he left Iroquois country, Lee never again saw his Seneca wife or his two children by the marriage. Years later, while he was campaigning in the Revolution, someone brought a report that his wife was alive and had inquired about him.

Lee returned to England in 1760. He then went to Portugal, where he campaigned with General John Burgoyne against the Spanish. While serving in this war, he distinguished himself in a valiant charge against the enemy. His service in the British army ended when he returned to England in 1762 and retired as a major with half pay. It has been thought that he failed to rise in the British army because of his offensive manners and his lack of concern for those upon whom his censure fell.[32]

Finding it difficult to live to his taste in London, Lee accepted a commission in the Polish army. As an aide-de-camp to King Stanislaus, he missed active duty and, weary of court life, accepted an appointment as the king's ambassador at Constantinople.[33] After returning to England in 1769, he again went to Poland, this time as a major general. With Russian allies, he fought against the Turks and subsequently toured central Europe. In Italy he killed an officer in a duel. He was fortunate enought to suffer only the loss of two fingers.[34]

By this time America had begun its historic controversy with the mother country over taxation. Lee at once became a partisan to the cause of liberty. He wrote from Poland to the earl of Charlemont: "I have, if possible, since my passage through Germany and my residence here, a greater horror of slavery than ever. For God's sake you patriot few at home, *principiis obstate*. . . . "[35] Poland, he held, was a country with a noble king and a vicious people, while England had a vicious king and a virtuous people. If they could but exchange kings, England would prosper by the deal.[36] To his sister, Lee again revealed his intense concern for American liberties: "May God prosper the Americans in their resolutions, that there may be one Asylum at least on the earth for men, who prefer their natural rights to the fantastical prerogative of a foolish perverted head because it wears a Crown."[37]

In 1773 Lee left England to make his home in America. During the first two years he lived wherever fancy led him. In 1774 he stayed with Washington for a while at Mount Vernon and then attended the First Continental Congress. Having a fair-sized fortune in England, in 1775 he borrowed $3,000 from Robert Morris and bought 2,800 acres in Berkeley County, Virginia. Since the barnlike house on his estate had but one big room, Lee drew chalk lines on the floor to map out the kitchen, bedroom, study, and *tack room*. "Sir," said Lee to a visitor, "it is the most convenient and economical establishment in the world. The lines of chalk which you see on the floor mark the division of the apartments, and I can sit in any corner, and give orders, or overlook the whole without moving my chair."[38]

As the outbreak of hostilities grew nearer, Lee intensified his attack on the British ministry. "As to North," he wrote to his friend General Thomas Gage at Boston, "my opinion of him is, (and I Have known him a long time), that did he hear of a single freeman in the remotest part of the World, he would willingly put his country to the expense of furnishing an army and fleet for the pleasure of destroying that single freeman." On the question of how and where America would find generals to fight a war, Lee countered by asking a friend, "What Generals have their tyrants? In fact, the match in this respect, will be pretty equal."[39]

When Lee attended the Second Continental Congress, almost every delegate regarded him as one of America's greatest assets in the struggle for constitutional rights. Like the others, Washington acknowledged that Lee was unsurpassed in military talent and in experience. Hamilton, who never liked Lee, observed in later years that he had "a certain pre-conceived and preposterous notion of his being a very great man," which always "operated in his favor."[40] When Congress, however, gave the command of the Continental army to Washington, Lee apparently felt no jealousy. Writing to Edmund Burke, he acknowledged the propriety of appointing a native American for the supreme command.[41] Nonetheless he expected to be made second-in-command and was disappointed when the position fell to Artemas Ward, a veteran of the French and Indian War, who had led the rebellious New Englanders in the siege of Boston. Lee spoke of Ward as the "fat old gentleman, who had been a popular church warden but had no acquaintance whatever with military affairs." This was an unfair appraisal of Ward, for although he was obese and almost too sick to head the troops, he had so far performed commendably as the commander in chief of the rebel forces.[42]

John Adams mirrored congressional thinking on army appoint-ments when he said that America had no one to compare with Lee (in his opinion one of the greatest generals in the world), but it would have been unwise to make anyone but a native American the commander in chief. As for Ward, Adams was of the opinion that he had the right to be second-in-command since he had served well and since Massachusetts was entitled to this honor. Lee was therefore left in third place, until Ward resigned in 1776 due to ill health.

When Washington and a retinue of officers who had been appoint-ed from the states south of New England reached Cambridge, Lee was given command of the Connecticut and Rhode Island forces in the Rox-bury area. From the outset, the clear-headed and likable Nathanael Greene, at the head of the Rhode Island men, was highly pleased with Lee, with his command of military science, and his ready wit and humor.

A visitor at Lee's headquarters aptly described him as "a Perfect original, a good scholar and soldier, and an odd genius, full of fire and passion, and but little good manners; a great sloven, wretchedly profane, and a great admirer of dogs." Indeed, he kept his favorite canines with him at all times. On one occasion, he astonished the quests at a dinner party by having his dog Spada mount a chair to offer a paw to Abigail Adams! As time passed and he grew in bitterness, he came to think that human beings as a race were as despicable as dogs were trustworthy and loyal.[43]

After the war started, Lee was one of the first to propose independence. "Unless you declare yourselves independent, establish a more certain and fixed legislature than that of a temporary courtesy of the people, you richly deserve to be enslaved," he told Edward Rutledge.[44]

When the British left Boston in the spring of 1776, Lee was sent to Charleston, South Carolina, to command the American forces in the South. His success in defending the city and beating off the enemy fleet came as one of the few bright spots for the American army during the year. Later, after the British were repulsed, Lee was called north to help Washington following the defeat on Long Island. He arrived in time to take part in the Battle of White Plains.

Late in October, fearing that an invasion of New Jersey would jeopardize the security of Philadelphia, Washington crossed the Hudson with the main army, leaving Lee and General William Heath to guard the Highlands and the approaches to New England. By November 14, Washington was at Hackensack, New Jersey; Greene occupied Fort Lee, directly opposite Fort Washington, at the northern end of Manhattan. Although nearly surrounded by the British, Fort Washington was still held by a garrison of nearly three thousand Americans.

Believing that Greene might be right in thinking that so long as the Americans held Fort Washington, Howe would not hazard an invasion of New Jersey, Washington hesitated to order an evacuation, although he realized the danger involved. Lee saw the mistake, but Washington continued to wait. Finally, on November 16, Howe sent his army from every possible direction against the doomed fort. The result was the capitulation of the entire garrison before the day was done.

The loss of nearly three thousand of some of the best troops in the American army was a stunning blow. Washington was to blame, but he was inclined to let the responsibility for the defeat fall on Greene. In an agonizing letter to Henry Knox, Greene poured out his anguish over the unfortunate turn of events. "I feel mad, vexed, sick, and sorry— never did I need the consoling voice of a friend more than now."[45]

The loss of Fort Washington prompted Lee's first outright criticism of Washington. To Joseph Reed he wrote: "I lament with you that fatal indecision of mind which in war is a much greater disqualification than stupidity or even want of personal courage. . ." Washington opened the letter by mistake and apoligized to Reed without further comment.[46] To Benjamin Rush, Lee wrote that he had predicted the loss of the fort unless the garrison was speedily withdrawn.[47]

Like Fort Washington, Fort Lee was taken by the British, who secretly scaled the palisades. Fortunately, Greene was warned in time to get his men over the Hackensack River and out of danger. Washington's prestige as a general was now falling fast and, conversely, Lee's fame soared. Reed expressed the feeling in the army and in Congress when he wrote to Lee:

I do not mean to flatter, nor praise you at the Expense of any other, but I confess I do think that it is entirely owing to you that this Army & the Liberties of America so far as they are dependent on it, are not totally cut off. You have Decision, a Quality often wanting in Minds otherwise valuable. . .[48]

The day after the fall of Fort Lee, Washington sent a note to Lee directing him to come to his aid in New Jersey. The order was discretionary, for it allowed Lee the option of staying longer in New York if he saw some "cogent reason" for doing so.[49] Since his force was depleted and a good share of the men had no shoes, Lee decided that it would be best to stay a while longer is search of supplies. A week later, he received another letter from Washington commending him for his efforts in gathering supplies and in collecting the Connecticut militia. He advised Lee to work out plans with the commissary for provisioning his troops when he started marching. Washington, although he was leaving Neward that morning with Cornwallis at his heels, conveyed no note of urgency.[50]

By the time the last note reached Lee, he had his troops readied for marching. The region between Peekskill and Morristown is hilly and rough, but Lee made good time and reached Morristown in about a week. At Morristown Lee learned that Washington might attempt to prevent Howe from crossing the Raritan at New Brunswick. Believing that he could best help by falling on the enemy's rear, Lee sent a message asking for orders. By the time the note arrived, Washington had given up trying to hold Howe at the Raritan and was marching for Trenton, where he would cross the Delaware. Accordingly he directed Lee to cross at one of the ferries above Trenton and meet him in Pennsylvania.[51]

Leaving Morristown, Lee marched his division to Basking Ridge. On the way, scouts were sent to the Delaware to search out a crossing. Lee, however, soon hit upon the stratagem of circling the British and marching to Burlington, where he would cross the Delaware. Lee thought he could strike British detachments at Princeton and cross the Delaware before Howe could overtake him. Besides his own division, he counted on the help of about a thousand New Jersey militia under Colonel Jacob Ford. Furthermore, General Gates, with three regiments, was coming from Ticonderoga to join him. Howe, himself, realized the potential danger of having a formidable body of American troops on his flank and rear.[52]

While Lee was spending the night at Mrs. White's tavern in Basking Ridge, his army camped two miles away. Lt. Colonel William Harcourt, who had served with Lee in Portugal, discovered Lee's whereabouts while he was scouting with a party of dragoons. After miles of traveling, Harcourt swooped down upon the tavern, took Lee prisoner, and carried his illustrious captive to New Brunswick, where the army celebrated the event all night long. In the course of the festivities even Lee's horse was made drunk by the exuberant officers.

At the very moment of his capture, Lee was in the process of writing a letter to General Gates. *"Entre Nous,"* wrote Lee, "a certain great man is most damnably deficient. He has thrown me into a situation where I have my choice of difficulties—if I stay in this Province, I risk myself and Army and if I do not stay the Province is lost for ever."[53]

Many writers have viewed Lee's conduct during Washington's retreat to Pennsylvania as tantamount to treason. However, a judicious appraisal of Lee's actions indicates that the charge is unjustified. Lee's first orders were discretionary, and he had good reasons for not marching immediately. When Washington's order finally became mandatory, Lee set his troops in motion and made good time considering the difficulties encountered. His plan of marching by way of Burlington, it should be noted, was to be executed only if Howe crossed the Delaware with his main force; it would seem to be within the scope of Washington's orders. Washington was informed of this plan by a letter from Lee on December 11; in it he said that he thought he could cross the "great Brunswick post-road" and by a forced march get over the Delaware by the ferry at Burlington."[54] During this maneuver he hoped to strike the detachments that Howe had left behind at Princeton and Trenton. Up until the time he was captured, therefore, no charges of misconduct, much less treason, could be made against him. His letter to Gates was highly critical of Washington, but there is no indication that he had any intention of disobeying the order to cross into Pennsylvania and join

Washington's force.

Prior to his exchange, Lee was transferred from New York to Philadelphia, where Howe soon granted him a parole to visit Congress at York, Pennsylvania. By this time Howe was in a much better frame of mind toward Lee and even apologized for any mistreatment he had suffered earlier.

After returning to Philadelphia, Lee found that his exchange had been confirmed and that he was free to report for duty at Valley Forge. Here he was given a hero's welcome by Washington and a coterie of officers, who rode out four miles to meet him and escort him into camp. After a sumptuous dinner party, Lee retired to the bedroom at Washington's headquarters. Then, as Elias Boudinot reports, he had a sergeant's wife brought to his chamber through a back door or window. The young woman, wrote Boudinot, was "a miserable dirty hussy" whom Lee had brought from Philadelphia. In the morning, when he finally appeared, dirty and disheveled as if he had slept in the street, Washington said nothing, although the noisy pair must have been overheard by both Martha and the general.[55]

Soon after Lee returned to the army, he asked Washington to see if he could do anything toward getting him a promotion. Some time before, Washington had advised Congress to create a higher rank than that of major general, but the legislators could not be made to see the need for it. When Lee found that all doors for promotion were closed, he was bitter. He partly blamed some of his fellow officers, who, he felt, were jealous of him. Greene, he heard, had advised Washington not to hurry his exchange. This may or may not have been true, but relations between the two men became strained and remained so until Greene set matters right with the disgruntled general.[56]

Before permitting Lee to resume his command in the army, Washington, as was the custom, had Lee take an oath of allegiance. While the oath was being administered, Lee withdrew his hand from the Bible. Noticing the action, Washington asked the reason for his strange behavior. Lee answered "As to King George, I am ready enough to absolve myself from all allegiance to him, but I have some scruples about the Prince of Wales." At that everyone laughed, assuming that Lee was indulging in another of his practical jokes.

This incident has been cited by many historians as additional proof that Lee was at heart a traitor. This, of course, is mere conjecture. A more plausible explanation may be that Lee acted as he did partly in jest and partly because he disliked all oaths of allegiance.[57]

Historians have also noted that Lee about this time reputedly told Joshua Loring that he hoped the Carlisle Commission would bring about reconciliation between Great Britain and the colonies. This may be true, but officers such as Daniel Morgan also were reported to favor reconciliation under terms acceptable to the colonies.[58]

While the agents for peace were in America, one of the commissioners, George Johnstone, got in touch with General Lee at Valley Forge. He told Lee that he hoped right-minded men on both sides could agree and secure an accommodation. Certainly Johnstone's letter evidences his sincere desire to see the mother country and her colonies once again united.

The great wish of my life is to see peace between two countries I almost equally love. . . . I meant. . . . to set before you many mutual advantages both would derive from an agreement: and as the terms now offered are more for the interest of your favorite America than you ever hoped to obtain, I should have made no scruple to ask your good offices, and to engage my own, to remove any obstacle that might obstruct the peace.[59]

Whether or not Lee answered this letter is not known, but he had already written to Johnstone complaining of the pillage and carnage committed by the British. Judging from Johnstone's letter, Lee had made no offer to aid the peace commission. Though formerly an advocate of reconciliation, Lee had apparently abandoned the hope that a union between the two countries could be effected.

When Lee returned to active service, the army was considered to be a powerful fighting force. Until late in the winter, the eleven hospitals at Valley Forge had been filled with sick and wounded. At one time nearly all of the four thousand men encamped there were reported sick—a very precarious situation for Washington had Howe decided to test his strength. As the spring advanced, however, the men recovered from their sicknesses, and new recruits arrived to help fill the ranks. These latter had the advantage of coming from well-provisioned homes and were generally strong and healthy. Furthermore, many of them had seen service before. By spring, too, Friedrich Wilhelm von Steuben had worked that amazing transformation of the army which excited universal admiration. From early dawn until late at night, the blustery German drilled the men until they were as proficient in arms as any European soldiers.

As the time for campaigning drew near, Washington began sounding out his officers on the best course to pursue. Most of them, Lee the most vociferous, were opposed to risking a general battle with an enemy still considered to be superior to the American army. On April 13, Lee wrote Washington that "a decisive action in fair Ground" was impossible. To assert otherwise "is talking Nonsense."[60]

For the most part the foreign officers sided with Lee, for they looked upon Clinton's army as decidedly superior to Washington's. Prominent among these was Brigadier General Louis Lebèque Duportail, a young officer who had been trained as an engineer in the French army. Cold and reserved in his manners, Duportail agreed with Lee that the Americans were no match for the British and that Washington should avoid a general action.[61]

When June 5 arrived and it was apparent that the British were about to leave Philadelphia, Lee wrote to Washington warning him against changing generals from one division to another at the beginning of or during a campaign. Washington answered that there was merit in Lee's suggestion but that he believed the officers were so well acquainted with all units that last minute changes would have no detrimental effect. Perturbed by so much advice from Lee, Washington let his lieutenant know that "The custom which many officers have, of speaking freely and reprobating measures, which upon investigation may be found to be unavoidable, is never productive of good, but often of very mischievous consequences."[62] Undoubtedly Washington was becoming annoyed.

In his correspondence, Lee also informed Washington that he believed Clinton would march toward New Castle and then turn and head for Lancaster in the hope of drawing the Americans into battle. Washington replied that he was aware of this possibility and that he had sent an engineer and three surveyors to study and map the area. He had also taken the precaution of having boats collected at points along the Susquehanna in case they were needed to transport the army over the river to avoid being trapped by the enemy.[63]

Washington called another council of war on June 17, the day before Clinton crossed the Delaware into New Jersey with his main army. As a whole the officers were still quite perplexed as to what the British would do. Some, influenced no doubt by Lee, thought they would go down the river and take a position in Delaware or Maryland. Greene, Lafayette, Wayne, Cadwallader, and Knox, however, seemed certain that Clinton would move directly to cross New Jersey and march for New York. But until the British actually started, they advised Washington to wait at Valley Forge. This he decided to do.[64]

II

The March to Monmouth

When Washington heard that General Clinton had evacuated Philadelphia, he immediately ordered the army to march to New Jersey to oppose the enemy. General Lee was commanded to lead the way with his division, which was to march for Coryell's Ferry, a few miles north of Trenton. Lee began marching from Valley Forge in the early morning of June 19, just as the British left Haddonfield to begin their march through New Jersey.[1]

By this time New Jersey militia were collecting to oppose the enemy. Soon more than a thousand militia were in the field ready to pounce upon any weak or exposed positions in the British columns. From the start there were also in New Jersey the New Jersey Continentals whom Washington had sent to Bordentown in May to cut off supplies going to Philadelphia and protect the area from enemy raids.[2]

The June of 1778 was unusually hot and rainy and from the beginning both sides experienced endless delays from flooded streams and muddy roads. During the march to Coryell's Ferry, Lee's troops were obliged to fill countless holes in the road with rails and boards and to assist the horses by pushing and tugging the heavily laden wagons. After two days of incessant toil by day and little rest at night, the troops reached the Delaware, where Durham boats awaited them. Swollen by the heavy rains, the Delaware was difficult to cross—a reminder of the ice-choked river during the attack on Trenton in 1776.[3]

Not long after the last of Lee's corps had crossed the Delaware,

Washington arrived at the river with the rest of the army. Upon conferring with Lee, he learned that the British had reached Mount Holly, where they had exchanged shots with some of the New Jersey militia and Continentals. The skirmish at Mount Holly was of short duration. The Americans disappeared not to give the enemy any more resistance until Bordentown was reached by the British left wing. Clinton was of the opinion that the Americans could have given him more trouble at Mount Holly since he had to breach a narrow pass where the rebels were well entrenched.[4]

Sir Henry Clinton, upon whom the command of the British army in America had fallen with General Howe's resignation, was forty years of age, stout, and of medium height. Since he was reputed to be a "hard, callous, aggressive soldier who understood war in its most brutal aspect," the conflict was expected to be conducted with more vigor and determination than before.[5] By nature he was reserved, with few of the qualities that excite admiration and esprit de corps. To a degree this was offset by his popularity among the Hessians, who remembered his services as an aide-de-camp for Ferdinand, duke of Brunswick, in the Seven Years' War and who were flattered by his fluency in German.

From the outset, Clinton was not pleased with a command faced by a retreat and with little prospect of victory with France, America's ally. "No officer," he wrote, "who had the least anxious regard for his professional fame would court a change so hopeless as this now appeared likely to be."[6]

Clinton's orders from London were to evacuate Philadelphia, which was no longer tenable with France as America's ally, and go to New York by sea. But he did not have enough transports for all the troops and the swarm of Loyalists begging to leave the city. To wait for more ships when it was known that a French fleet was on the way to America would be perilous. Clinton was also mindful that if he went by sea and experienced unfavorable winds, Washington by a swift move might descend upon New York, which was defended by a garrison of only four thousand troops. Considering all, Clinton estimated that he could cross New Jersey in a matter of two or three weeks. With ten thousand of the finest soldiers in the world, he entertained no fear from Washington during the march.[7]

During the turmoil accompanying the evacuation of Philadelphia the British took time to celebrate King George's birthday. The rejoicing, however, had a hollow ring. The very thought of quitting Philadelphia and beating a retreat was as repugnant to the whole army as it was to General Clinton. Most of the British officers, including Sir William Erskine and Major General Charles Grey, believed that Washington's army could be defeated in Pennsylvania. There was no reason therefore for retreating through New Jersey like an army on the run. Furthermore, they were aware that an ignominious retreat would undermine the morale of Loyalists everywhere in America and cause them to feel that they no longer could depend on the British for protection.[8]

There was one consolation in Clinton's decision to march overland to New York. Washington's army or part of it might be drawn into battle. The Americans were stronger, Clinton admitted, than ever before, but he was as confident as his officers they would be no match for his dauntless regulars. That the militia and some Continentals had given up their post at Mount Holly and beaten a hasty retreat strengthened the British in their opinion that the march through New Jersey would not be hazardous.

While at Coryell's Ferry, Washington strengthened the forces confronting the enemy by reinforcing them with some of his best soldiers. Colonel Daniel Morgan's rangers, with others picked from the regiments for their marksmanship, were the first to go. Soon Colonel Stephen Moylan was dispatched with his light horse to help impede the enemy.

Word presently came to Washington that Moylan was operating on the enemy's front while a detachment of light horse under Colonel Anthony Walton White was on the left flank of the advancing Redcoats. Considering, however, that few skirmishes were reported, it would seem that the American cavalry kept a respectful distance from the British line and its powerful contingent of dragoons.

As Washington's army trudged along the rain-soaked roads in the effort to head off the British, Major General Nathanael Greene labored to keep supplies moving and prepare the army for battle. Much of his work had been done weeks before the opening of the campaign, when he struggled to collect supplies scattered at government depots throughout Pennsylvania and Maryland.

On the march Greene's corps belonging to the quartermaster department was constantly employed. Artisans were kept busy repairing wagons, harnesses, guns, and equipment of all kinds. No one was busier than Colonel Clement Biddle, the foragemaster, who scoured the countryside for fodder for the thousands of horses belonging to the army.

Greene himself overlooked no details which might slow down the army or impair its fighting power. Every day he picked campsites with water, good drainage, and defensive ground. When the troops arrived, they found latrines, firewood, and piles of straw for bedding. Springs were walled with stone to keep the water from becoming muddy from constant use. Barrels of vinegar were provided for warding off intestinal disorders.

Although Washington's route to Monmouth was considerably longer than Clinton's, the British advance was slower. Their wagon train, ten miles long, carried tons of baggage as well as provisions for the army and grain for the horses. The army consumed over thirty tons of food each week, and not being sure how long it might take to cross New Jersey, Clinton ordered provisions enough for six weeks. For a time Clinton considered destroying much of the excess baggage, but since such an action might be taken as a sign of weakness, he put the thought aside. Afterward he admitted that it had been a mistake regardless of the fact that he did not lose a single wagon during the entire march.

Clinton's army was in fine condition when it left Philadelphia; it had had good care during the winter with plenty of exercise from marching, combating rebel raiding parties, and working on redoubts. Weaker men could never have carried eighty-pound packs, sweltered in heavy woolen clothes, and survived the hardships of the march. Swarms of mosquitoes tormented the soldiers, whose only protection was their heavy clothing. For hours the troops were pelted with heavy rain, but even the rain was preferable to the sweltering heat that followed the showers. Pauses caused by rain, breakdowns in the wagon trains, bridges destroyed, and trees felled across the roads by daring rebels, no doubt saved many men from total exhaustion.

During the first week of the march, Clinton lost by desertion about five hundred men, fully as many as would be lost in battle during the entire campaign. Most of the deserters were Hessians who returned to Philadelphia, where wives or sweethearts awaited them among the German population.

For the first forty miles Clinton's army advanced in two main divisions with Lord Cornwallis leading the main column and taking the highway to Allentown, New Jersey. On the way his troops marveled at the "great forests of gnarled chestnut and swamp maples." Trailing Cornwallis came General Wilhelm von Knyphausen with several brigades of Hessians acting as a guard for the seemingly endless caravan.[9]

The other division, led by General Alexander Leslie, followed a road nearer the Delaware. Each regiment marched to the music of fifes and drums, though the Royal Artillery outdid all others, with a band of two trumpets, two french horns, two bassoons, and four clarinets. Clinton's entire army was guarded by six or seven hundred well-mounted dragoons scattered along the sides of the advancing columns.[10]

At Bordentown, Leslie's division encountered an ambuscade at a drawbridge where militia contested the crossing. This time the British had only to bring a cannon or two into play before the militia precipitously withdrew. Further on, dragoons under Colonel John G. Simcoe, who accompanied Leslie, with flashing sabers charged at and dispersed a body of milita at a ford.[11]

The hardest-fought skirmish occurred when Simcoe's Rangers ran into a large contingent of Continentals and militia at Crosswicks. The Americans had placed themselves defensively at points along the rise on the eastern bank of the creek. Below them the bridge was but partly demolished, so rapid was the advance of the enemy. While the British artillery bombarded the American position, Simcoe's horsemen charged across the stream in a hail of bullets from American muskets. During the skirmish the British had four killed and several wounded. The Americans suffered less since they fired once or twice and then vanished.[12] Two or three cannonballs fired by the British can still be seen imbedded in the walls of the old Quaker meetinghouse above the creek.

On June 24, after about a week of marching, Clinton reached the tiny hamlet of Allentown, where he was forced to decide whether to try to reach New York by way of Amboy or take the longer route to Sandy Hook, whence transports could carry his army to New York. After weighing the alternatives, he decided that the Amboy route posed too many dangers. Washington's army, then at Hopewell near Princeton, was nearer to Amboy than his own and could attack him while his army was crossing the Raritan River. In addition, with General Horatio Gates marching to join Washington from the north, the odds might become unfavorable if he chose to go to Amboy.

In choosing Sandy Hook, Clinton reasoned that his army, after it reached Middletown, would have the protection of high ground and the waters of New York Bay and the Atlantic Ocean on its flanks. Furthermore, there would remain the possibility of drawing Washington into a general battle in an area favorable to the British. Should he give Washington a sound beating, even though he did not destroy his army, British prestige would be appreciably restored, and he would gain honor at the very outset of taking command.[13]

On leaving Allentown, Knyphausen was put in the lead with the baggage train. The rest of the army was thus placed between the long and vulnerable line of supplies and the oncoming Americans. On the night of June 25, Clinton's army lay camped for several miles along the roadside near Imlayton. On the afternoon of the next day, it reached Freehold. Here the tired troops rested while officers lounged in their tents, drank wine, and studied maps.

When Washington reached Hopewell, he called a council of war (on a day, incidentally, when there occurred an almost complete eclipse of the sun). For some time Greene and like-minded officers had been pressing him to send out more troops against the enemy. With good reasons, however, Washington had refused to commit more men until he knew whether Clinton was headed for Amboy or Sandy Hook. Now it appeared that the latter was his destination, and he agreed to send Brigadier General Charles Scott forward with fifteen hundred men to aid the troops near the enemy.[14]

During the discussions at the council of war, Lee and several supporters continued to insist that nothing was to be gained by detaching more troops for action near the enemy's lines. As he did earlier, he talked of the wisdom of making a "bridge of gold" over which Clinton could pass to New York. Again he emphasized the fact that France was now America's ally and that an American defeat could do much harm, while a victory, unless it was a great one, would accomplish little.[15] As it turned out, the detachments after they were placed under Lafayette's command accomplished nothing. They could have met with a defeat which would have crippled Washington's army.

Since the advanced corps would number about thirty-five hundred Continentals counting Morgan's rangers, the New Jersey Continentals, and Scott's brigade, it seemed imperative to have an officer in charge of all the units in the field. Lee, as senior general, had the right of command, but since he regarded it as too weak a force to do much more than trail the enemy, he considered it as beneath his dignity. Washington thereupon offered the command to Lafayette, who accepted it enthusiastically.[16]

The decision to reinforce the advanced troops with Scott's brigade still found Greene and like-minded officers dissatisfied. A stronger force near the enemy was needed, they insisted. In a letter to Washington, Greene defined his thoughts:

I am not for hazarding a general action unnecessarily, but I am clearly of opinion for making a serious impression with the light troops and for having the Army in supporting distance. As I said yesterday in council, I would have two Brigades to support them. The attack should be made on the English flank and rear. . . . If we suffer the enemy to pass through New Jersey without attacking, I think we shall every regret it. I cannot help thinking we magnify our *deficiences* beyond realities. . . . People expect something from us and our strength demands it. I am by no means for rash measures, but we must preserve our reputation. . . .[17]

Brigadier General Anthony Wayne, who habitually favored aggressive action, agreed with Greene. Although a general battle should be avoided unless circumstances presaged success, more troops, he insisted, should be sent forward.[18] A powerful force near the enemy might find an opportunity to inflict a telling blow against the British. All the hawks among the Americans believed the tendency was to underrate the Continentals. Among the enemy, too, there were officers who had acquired respect for the American soliders. Wrote the Hessian Major Baurmeister, "They are bold, unyielding, and fearless. They have an abundance of that something which urges them on and cannot be stopped."[19]

Not long after Scott's brigade was sent out, Greene and Hamilton reputedly went to Washington to urge him to send more troops to the advanced corps. "I know what you have come for," Washington is reported to have said on seeing them. It may be that he had just decided to detach more troops, for after some discussion he said that he would send Wayne forward with his battle-tried Pennsylvania troops and with some equally good Connecticut men—in all, about a thousand.[20]

Exhilarated by the thought that he might soon win glory on the field of battle, Lafayette took command of the advanced troops on June 25. His orders were to "take the first opportunity to attack the rear of the enemy," and he lost no time in attempting to carry out his instructions.[21] Washington, however, on second thought sensed the danger of having so zealous an officer in command and sent him a word of caution. "Tho giving the Enemy a stroke," he wrote, "is a very desirable event, yet I would not wish you to be too precipitate in the measure or to distress your men by an over hasty march. The Weather is extremely warm and by a too great exertion in pushing Troops, many will fall sick and be rendered entirely unfit for Service."[22]

The day after Lafayette joined the advanced troops, Washington directed Colonel Alexander Hamilton to join the marquis as adviser and aide-de-camp. Hamilton was then twenty-seven, eight years older than Lafayette. Since 1777, he had been one of Washington's aides. His critical turn of mind often irritated Washington, who nevertheless recognized the young man's ability and seldom failed to listen to his opinions. All during the council of war at Hopewell, Hamilton chaffed at the indecision and caution of most of the officers. Greene and Wayne were of one mind with Hamilton when the latter spoke of the "imbecility of a council of war." The Hopewell meeting, declared Hamilton, "would have done honor to the most honorable society of midwives and them only."[23]

On June 26, with the enemy near Imlayton, Lafayette wrote Washington that he and his staff had decided to march during the night and attack the enemy's rear guard in the morning. Wayne's troops together with the New Jersey brigade under Brigadier General William Maxwell, he said, were already advancing.

Only a few hours after Washington received Lafayette's message, he received disconcerting news from Hamilton, who had just arrived at Lafayette's camp. Wayne's troops, he reported, were out of food and too famished to march against the enemy. With the heavy rains and so many detachments to look after, Greene had been unable to forward supplies and provisions fast enough.

More disconcerting, perhaps, was Hamilton's report that American intelligence was very poor. Most, if not all, of Moylan's horses were ahead of the British and not in communication with Lafayette. The marquis had some mounted militia, but none of these were operating between the lines to gather information. Most of the horses belonging to the militia were in fact too worn out to be of much service. Lafayette not only did not have any accurate knowledge of the whereabouts of the enemy but did not even know where some of his detachments were located. Still more amazing, he had no knowledge of where Washington was with the main army. In an effort to learn where the British were as well as where some of the American detachments were to be found, Hamilton rode all night but returned to Lafayette's headquarters with scant information.[24]

In a second letter to Washington, Hamilton correctly estimated the situation facing Lafayette. "To attack them in their situation, without being supported by the whole army would be folly in the extreme," he wrote. Since Washington was not in supporting distance, Hamilton knew that there was danger of losing the entire advance corps. The poor generalship shown during this time was Washington's as well as Lafayette's. If Clinton had not been so preoccupied with getting his baggage away, he might have exploited the opportunity to attack and annihilate one detachment after another.[25]

Following his disconcerting reports from Hamilton, Washington received a message from Lafayette saying that he was advancing, even though he was desperately short of provisions. Hamilton and others, he said, were out looking for Scott—who, he hoped, would join him at Hidestown. As for the enemy, he admitted he did not know their exact location but assumed that they were in the direction of Freehold. This disturbing letter was followed by another that made Washington somewhat relieved. Lafayette wrote that he had now been forced to call off the advance since the men were too famished and exhausted to go any further.[26]

As soon as Washington learned of Lafayette's dangerous course, he sent out a rider with orders to turn northward away from the enemy and take a position near Englishtown. Here he could find provisions and be supported by the main army. This order reached Lafayette immediately after he had called a halt to his feverish attempt to engage the British. Some of Lafayette's advanced troops actually did get within a mile of the enemy lines at Freehold before being called back.[27]

Upon receiving the order to march to Englishtown, Lafayette was filled with disappointment. The order, he thought, had cost him a great opportunity to win fame and glory. Amazingly enough, he did not see the necessity of marching the eleven miles to Englishtown, never realizing, it would seem, the danger he was in without the support of the main army.[28]

In commenting upon Lafayette's generalship, "Light Horse" Henry Lee in later years said that the marquis was unskilled in the art of war. He refrained, however, from criticizing Washington for giving him the command, probably out of respect for the commander in chief.[29] It might be thought that some of the officers at the time would have questioned the wisdom of putting so many troops in the care of a youth. The officers were reluctant, however, to question Washington's decisions, especially when a favorite such as the marquis was involved.

Not long after Wayne had left for the advanced division and Lafayette had assumed command, General Lee underwent a change of mind. Counting all units, the advanced corps had become a very respectable body—one which, as second in command, he should be leading. In a letter to Washington, he summed up the matter:

When I first assented to the Marquis de Lafayette's taking the command of the present detachment, I confess I viewed it in a very different light from that in which I view it at present. I considered it as a more proper business of so young, volunteering general, than of the second in command of the army; but I find it is considered in a different manner. They say that a corps consisting of six thousand men, the greater part chosen, is undoubtedly the most honorable command next to the Commander-in-Chief; that my ceding it would of course have an odd appearance.[30]

Stirling, who was next in rank, agreed with Lee. It would be a reflection on the senior officers, the latter declared, if Lafayette held the command.

Recognizing the validity of the claim, Washington was quite perplexed; he probably realized that he should have consulted Lee when Wayne's brigade was added to those with Lafayette. After pondering the matter for some time, Washington found a way out of his dilemma by sending Lee forward with two brigades to take over the command, with the understanding that Lafayette could carry out any operation already started: a rather risky provision considering Lafayette's craving for military glory and the dangers confronting the advanced division. In any event, Lafayette received the arrangements as face-saving enough, and his need for provisions made it impossible to tangle with the enemy before marching to Englishtown.[31]

It was the afternoon of June 27, the day before the Battle of Monmouth, when Lafayette arrived at Englishtown to turn over his division to Lee. Three or four miles to the west toward Cranbury was Washington's main army. Up beyond the Tennent Meeting House, three miles east of Englishtown and not far from the enemy's outposts, was Major

General Philemon Dickinson with his New Jersey militia. Protected by swampy ground and the Middle Spotswood Brook, the militia formed the advanced guard; Simcoe's Rangers were only about a mile away near Freehold.

The eight or nine hundred New Jersey men with Dickinson had performed praiseworthy services in doggedly doing their utmost to slow down the advance of the British. Their efforts, along with those of Morgan's riflemen, Moylan's horse, and Maxwell's Continentals, had at least made it possible for Washington to catch up with the enemy. The two armies were now posed for battle.

Behind Simcoe's advanced position the British army lay camped for several miles along the Allentown-Middletown road. Cornwallis's troops occupied the section west of Freehold, while Knyphausen's men with the baggage extended eastward from the little village of Freehold. All were on high defensive ground where streams and swamps shielded the army in the direction of the Americans.

By staying at Freehold all day Saturday, June 27, Clinton clearly was inviting battle with his adversary. He did not have to stay there; one day's march would have put his army on the high ground at Middletown, where the British would have been safe from attack.

During the rest at Freehold, Clinton's engineers busied themselves mapping the roads to Middletown and Sandy Hook. Meanwhile, the weather remained hot and humid, and there were showers. During the day several houses were burned—in spite of Clinton's reassertion that he would shoot anyone found destroying property. For amusement some troops pulled down the bell from Saint Peter's Episcopal Church; but for the most part the day was too warm to encourage pranks or acts of vandalism.[32]

While the British lay camped at Freehold, Morgan was keeping a close watch on their right only a few miles away. In one instance a party of his rangers, aided by some of Washington's handsomely-dressed guards, surprised and captured fifteen grenadiers bathing in a stream. When the men reported to camp with their prisoners, Morgan was convulsed with laughter at seeing the splendid uniforms of the guards, whom he called "the gentlemen," all spattered with mud.[33]

In numbers the two armies were fairly equal. In all, Clinton had about ten thousand regulars and three thousand provincials. Washington had more, perhaps twelve thousand Continentals and two thousand militia and irregulars. But as John Watts De Peyster, a Civil War general, once said, "No war horse ever counted his militia as effectives."[34]

As to the fighting potential of the two armies, most officers at the time, whether British or American, still considered the British the better soldiers. Besides their crack grenadiers, Fort Guards, Hessian yagers, and light infantry, the British dragoons could be very effective on the rolling plains of Freehold. In contrast, the American army, which always had a large number of new recruits, was untested despite Steuben's training. Monmouth would be the proving ground.[35]

III

Lee's Advance and Retreat

As he had been directed by Washington, Lee held a staff meeting in the late afternoon of Saturday, June 27. At it were the brigadiers William Maxwell, Charles Scott, Anthony Wayne, and Lafayette, who held the rank of major general. There were also Lee's aides: Lieutenant Colonel John Brooks, Colonel Marquis Francis de Malmedy, Major John Francis Mercer, Major George L. Turberville, and Captain Evan Edwards. All together, Lee's circle of officers and aides made a competent and reliable group.

Wayne was known for his daring and for his willingness to hazard a battle on almost any occasion. William Maxwell, called "Scotch Willie," resigned from the British army at the beginning of the war to lead a New Jersey regiment. Charles Scott, a brigadier general of the Virginia line since 1777, was thirty-nine. Although all but forgotten in history, he was hardly less colorful than the mercurial Wayne. As a youth of seventeen, Scott had served under Washington during the disastrous Braddock campaign of 1755. After the Revolution, he became a judge and one of the early governors of Kentucky. In 1794, he was again in uniform, this time serving with Wayne in the Battle of Fallen Timber against the Indians of the Northwest. Before the Battle of Monmouth ended both Wayne and Scott became severe critics of General Lee's performance.

Among the aides, Major John Francis Mercer was a graduate of William and Mary; he became a governor of Maryland in later years. As

Virginians, the Mercers, who came from Scotland, soon emerged as one of the foremost families of the Dominion. During the Stamp Act crisis, Mercer's older brothers, James and George, fought bitterly with Richard Henry Lee and his brothers, all of whom were accused by the Mercers of being too friendly to the British point of view.[1] Now only nineteen, Major Mercer was an ardent admirer of General Lee, who, incidentally, was no relation to the Lee family of Virginia. After the Battle of Monmouth, Mercer resigned from the army, ostensibly because he resented the abuse heaped upon Lee.

Like Mercer, Captain Evan Edwards was a rather learned young man, another of Lee's favorites. Later in the war, he served as an aide-de-camp to General Greene in the South. According to Greene, Edward's flair for strange doctrines and "singular sentiments" gave rise to innumerable arguments between the young man and his companions.[2] The twenty-six year old Lieutenant Colonel John Brooks had left a medical career in Massachusetts to join the army. Colonel Malmedy, a French volunteer, later in the war led a troop of horse with Greene in the Southern campaign.

Lee explained to his officers that Washington wanted the advanced corps to march early in the morning and, if possible, to attack the enemy's rear. Since there was no exact information as to where the several units of the British army were camped and little knowledge of the topography in the direction of the enemy, it was difficult to determine how to move against the enemy. Much would depend on what the British did and what the ground would be like when the Americans approached the enemy. Lee did, however, ask his officers not to quibble over rank and placement and to carry out the orders as best they could when the march began. Maxwell had seniority among the brigadiers, but since he had many new recruits, it was decided that he would bring up the rear.[3]

During the night, Lee had little or no sleep. Surrounded as usual by several of his pet dogs, he talked with members of his staff, who themselves were apparently too exhilarated to sleep. As usual, Edwards and Mercer hung on every word spoken by the old warrior. He was, indeed, a fascinating conversationalist, especially since his vocabulary and mannerisms were those of the highest military school. As he talked, he punctuated his observations with wit and sarcasm to the delight of his listeners.[4]

About one in the morning, after receiving instructions from Washington, Lee notified Dickinson and Morgan that he would be marching early in the morning as soon as guides were found and that they should be ready to aid him by attacking the enemy's flanks. Dickinson was also ordered to send forward immediately from his base at the Tennent Meeting House several hundred men to watch the enemy and gather information. The messages were sent at two A.M., since Edwards remembered looking at his watch when the riders left.[5]

At about four in the morning, Lafayette, who apparently could get no more sleep than the others, paid Lee a visit and asked if there was anything he could do. Lee told Lafayette that instructions had just been received from Washington directing him to send forward six hundred Continentals to back up Dickinson's men. The troops were now preparing to leave, he said, under the command of Colonel William Grayson of the Viginia line. Lee also informed Lafayette that he would command the select troops consisting of the brigades under Wayne and Scott. The assignment pleased Lafayette, who, as second in command, was entitled to lead the corps.[6]

The first dispatch Lee received from Dickinson came at about five o'clock. It reported that the enemy's advanced division under Knyphausen had begun marching. Lee then sent another message to Grayson asking him to move out without further delay. Grayson began marching at once and reached Englishtown shortly after daybreak. Here he was held up again for nearly half an hour while General David Forman hunted for guides.[7]

Grayson, upon whom fell the honor of leading the attack, was a forty-two-year-old Virginian; he had attended the College of Philadelphia and studied law in London. At the outbreak of the war, he was practicing law in Virginia. After joining the Continental army, he rose rapidly and became colonel in 1777, after serving for a time as one of Washington's aides-de-camp. Like Lee, he was considered a great conversationalist, skilled in debate, and admired for his wit and humor.

After Lee had relayed the message from Dickinson that the British were marching, Washington sent an order to Lee to attack. He was to advance as fast as possible and attack the enemy's rear "unless there should be powerful reasons to the contrary."[8] These were the words given in testimony by Lt. Colonel Richard Kidder Meade, an aide-de-camp for Washington, who raced astride his famed black horse to deliver the message to Lee at the first morass. Lee interpreted the message to mean that he was to attack unless he believed it inadvisable to do so for military reasons. The order in his mind was clearly discretionary in nature.

Another aide, Major John Clark, carried a second message from Washington directing Lee to attack the enemy. "You will inform General Lee," Clark testified of the message he carried, "that 'tis my orders he annoy the Enemy as much as in his power, but at the same time to proceed with caution and take care the Enemy don't draw him into a scrape." This order was sent an hour or so after Meade had delivered his message. Major Clark did not find Lee until noon, when he came upon him near Freehold, after his division had retreated from the third morass. According to Clark, he called Lee aside and delivered the orders "which I did and still do conceive to be discretionary and as such he received them."[9] Ironically the message arrived just after Lee's division came close to getting into a "scrape"; now, however, Lee had begun a retrograde movement that would carry him out of danger.

Letters written by Washington during the time the orders were being sent to Lee also show that the commander in chief did not want a general battle and that Lee's orders were indeed discretionary. In a letter to General Gates written at six in the morning, Washington said that the army was pressing forward and that he intended "to harass them as much as possible."[10] Later, at seven o'clock, he wrote President Laurens that he had ordered Lee to "attack their rear if possible."[11]

The record is therefore clear that Lee was not ordered to attack under all circumstances; he was given authority to determine whether conditions were favorable or unfavorable for battle. In other words, it was left for him to decide whether to attack or not. As William Gordon, the historian, concluded: "Lee could not consider them [the orders] as requiring him to risk a general engagement, in direct repugnancy to the spirit of those councils of war that had been repeatedly held on the subject."[12]

After guides were found, Grayson marched two miles to the Tennent Meeting House. Here he found some of Dickinson's militia scattered in parties to guard the roads. Some were down the main road in the direction of Freehold, where Dickinson had stationed his advanced post in accordance with Washington's instructions.[13]

When Grayson reached the causeway over the Middle Spotswood Brook, firing broke out up ahead where Dickinson had placed some men on the rise beyond the brook. It was then seven-thirty, the air already hot and sticky. Fearing that the milita were in trouble, Grayson ordered his detachment forward, leaving Dickinson at the bridge for support. One artillery officer told of climbing the rise and pointing a cannon at the enemy, apparently a large body of dragoons.

Whether or not Grayson was aware of it, the Americans were being attacked by Simcoe and his hussars, who had camped not far away. Before Grayson's men had a chance to exchange fire with their adversary, word came that they were in danger of being surrounded by a large body of the enemy. Believing that the report might be true and having been warned by Dickinson not to rely on the militia, Grayson immediately retired to the bridge. The enemy did not pursue, and soon all the green-coated hussars, in reality not a substantial force, were out of sight.[14]

Leaving their packs behind, Lee moved his division about an hour after Grayson had left Englishtown. Wayne led the way with Scott, Jackson, and Maxwell following. Riding ahead of the marching men, Lee and his staff reached the bridge over the brook about the time Grayson pulled back to the protection of the stream and the surrounding morass.

Going immediately to General Dickinson, Lee was informed that by the latest report the British had not left Freehold. It would be very dangerous to advance, Dickinson emphatically declared, until it was certain the enemy was marching and not drawn up ready for battle. "General Lee," Dickinson is quoted as saying, "you may believe me or not, but if you march your party beyond the ravine now in your rear, which has only one passage over it, you are in a perilous situation."[15]

Lee saw the merit in Dickinson's advice but seemed anxious to go after the enemy as Washington had ordered. He waited for nearly an hour at the bridge while contradictory reports came in one after another. Some were that the British were moving off, others that they were still at Freehold, while still others were that the enemy was actually marching toward Lee with flanking columns.[16]

While Lee waited impatiently at the bridge, troops were marched over the brook but were then recalled as one report conflicted with another. Finally, Lieutenant Colonel John Laurens, the son of President Laurens, who had been reconnoitering with Malmedy and a troop of horses, came in to report that to all appearances the enemy had left

Freehold and were marching toward Middletown. Lee then made up his mind to advance regardless of Dickinson, who wanted him to wait longer and with whom he had had some sharp words regarding the reliability of the information furnished by the militia.[17]

It appears that baron von Steuben was with Laurens during reconnoitering of the enemy lines. Writing to his father, he remarked that Steuben came narrowly close to being captured by the enemy. Steuben, his son, and several others, it seems, came so close to the British that either Clinton or Cornwallis recognized him by his Silver Star of the Order of Fidelity and ordered the dragoons to capture him. He escaped by racing his horse, losing only his hat in the mad race for safety. In another account, Von Eelking, a Hessian officer, claims that Knyphausen, an old friend of Steuben's, recognized him, commanded his men not to fire, and saved the general's life.[18] This version of the episode seems less likely to be true, unless the encounter happened on June 27, as some authors have held. On either day, however, Knyphausen was beyond Freehold in an area where American scouting parties would not ordinarily penetrate. When Laurens made his approach to the enemy's lines, Knyphausen had been marching for several hours and was far beyond Freehold.

While Lee waited at the bridge, Lafayette appeared with the whole division. The regiments with Jackson and Grayson were now added to Wayne's Pennsylvanians, which would lead the advance. Wayne's vanguard was commanded by Lieutenant Colonel Richard Butler. Born in Ireland, Butler had migrated with his father to Pennsylvania, where he became involved in the fur trade with the Indians. During the Pontiac uprising, he served with Colonel Henry Bouquet and fought in the bloody battle with the Indians at Bushy Run. He joined the Continental army early in the Revolution and, at Saratoga, served with distinction as one of Morgan's lieutenants commanding the hard-bitten riflemen. After the Revolution, he lost his life fighting the Indians in Indiana. At Monmouth, though he was only thirty-five, he was regarded as a veteran warrior.

As Butler led his men along the sandy road that led past Craig's house and then in the direction of the courthouse, some of the soldiers were already staggering from the effects of the heat and humidity. After passing through a defile, the troops emerged on the high ground where the Queen's Rangers had camped the night before. It was nine-thirty, not a leaf stirring. Then all at once in front of Butler loomed a body of dragoons forming for a charge.

Butler, who had some horse (probably Lieutenant Colonel George Baylor's troop), had just time enough to form a line when the enemy with flashing sabers came charging upon the Pennsylvanians. "Fire!" shouted Butler. One volley from several hundred muskets and two cannon was enough. After firing their pistols with more noise than effect, the charging horsemen—Simcoe's hussars and some dragoons of the Sixteenth Regiment—whirled about and galloped out of range.[19]

So swiftly did the hussars fall back that they came racing upon Cornwallis's guards and grenadiers, who were themselves thrown into wild confusion. That the latter were still in Freehold proves that Dickinson was right when he warned Lee that the enemy were there. During the brief encounter Simcoe and several others on the British side were wounded. Injured in the arm, Simcoe was forced to report to the hospital, and the command of the Rangers passed to a Captain Ross.[20] In Freehold today a monument stands to commemorate the spot where this first action took place between the Continentals and the enemy.

Although Lieutenant Colonel John Graves Simcoe (the future lieutenant governor of Canada) was at this time only twenty-six, he had reorganized and trained one of the best outfits in the British army. He had become commander of the Rangers in 1777, after Major James Wemyss was wounded at Germantown. Among the companies he raised was one composed of Highland Scots, complete with kilts and bagpipes. By the beginning of the 1778 campaign, Simcoe had eight companies, one of them a corps of grenadiers celebrated for their height and physical powers. At first he had no cavalry, but he soon raised a troop of hussars who were considered to be as good as any horsemen in America.[21]

The British cavalry, like the American, it should be noted, seldom charged pell-mell upon an enemy unless it seemed quite certain that their prey would break, scatter, and fall to the mercy of saber-swinging horsemen. Otherwise, if their opponents stood fast and kept firing, the horsemen would fly away to avoid heavy losses in a rain of bullets. Such was the case in this instance: Simcoe's hussars wisely turned about and fell back to the protection of Cornwallis's infantry.

To verify the report that Cornwallis was leaving Freehold, Lafayette presently rode forward to reconnoiter. After crossing a marsh, called the third morass, that bordered the village on the east, he came in view of Briar's Hill and the woods and fields surrounding it. In the distance he saw what he was looking for: Cornwallis's marching column and behind it a large body of dragoons on the Middletown road.

As soon as Lee received Lafayette's report, he ordered his division to cross a causeway over the morass and form along the rim of the ravine. By ten o'clock, all of Lee's troops were over the morass except Maxwell's New Jersey brigade, which had been left behind as reserves in the woods atop a nearby hill. One soldier described how his regiment followed the road through a deep ravine and came out on a field of Indian corn facing Briar's Hill: "The sun was shining full upon the field, the soil of which was sandy, the mouth of a heated oven seemed to me to be but a trifle hotter than this ploughed field, it was almost impossible to breathe."[22]

While Lee's infantry was assembling and being posted in battle formation, the twenty-three-year-old Lieutenant Colonel Eleazer Oswald, in command of the artillery, selected a knoll at the edge of an orchard and began firing his cannon at the enemy collecting on Briar's Hill. Oswald's men unquestionably had the most fatiguing work of all. Stripped to their waists, they were on the verge of fainting as they feverishly manned the cannons. Two were killed when a British cannonball came tearing through their ranks. Among those commanding Oswald's brave band of artillerymen were such fearless officers as Captain Sebastian Bauman and Captain Thomas Bliss, the latter destined to be captured by the British during Lee's retreat.[23]

Born in England, Oswald had served with Arnold and Ethan Allen in the capture of Ticonderoga in 1775. Later, during the ill-fated Canadian campaign, he acted as Arnold's secretary. During and after the Revolution, few Americans fought more duels than the pugnacious Oswald. who seldom failed to kill his opponent. After the war, his ardor for the revolutionary cause in France led him to join the Republican army. He returned to America after the Reign of Terror led him to change his mind about the French Revolution. Like Captain Edwards, he remained devoted to Lee, who he thought was pilloried solely for daring to demand an apology from Washington.

By the time Lee had crossed the third morass, Knyphausen's division was several miles beyond Freehold, his long caravan snaking along the road to Middletown. As he surveyed the situation, Clinton was not at all worried about Cornwallis with six thousand of the best troops in the British army. But he was very concerned about the baggage with Knyphausen. Moylan's horse and any number of mounted militia were hovering over the baggage ready to pounce on any wagons that appeared vulnerable. While watching his prey, Moylan sent Washington a note with the assurance that he was doing all in his power to frustrate the enemy's march. "They are now again in motion," he wrote at two-thirty in the afternoon,

and seem to bend their course towards Middletown, through by-woods which were not suspected to be passable, but there are so many intersections in the roads that it is impossible to judge whether they will go to Middletown or on to the falls. I have them full in view, and we must move as a party is endeavoring to surround me.[24]

Concerned as he was about his baggage train, Clinton was confident that Knyphausen could defend it unless Lee swung around Cornwallis and struck a sudden blow at the caravan. In all, Knyphausen had about four thousand troops, consisting of two battalions of crack light infantry and equally superb Hessian yagers. In addition, he had two brigades of British regulars and the brigades of Stirne's and Loos's Hessians, as well as the Pennsylvania, Maryland, and West Jersey volunteers. To round out his force, he had the Seventeenth Regiment of Dragoons, nearly three hundred horsemen.

Besides being well-protected, Knyphausen did not have to worry about his horses since the British had picked up along the line of march hundreds of horses for replacement. They had also taken all the cattle and sheep they could find, paying for them in cash as they went along.[25]

While studying the enemy's position on Briar's Hill, Lee hit upon a bold course. By circling to the left with the main part of his division, he could get behind the British rear guard while the remainder of his corps attacked in front. Lieutenant Colonel David Rhea, of the New Jersey line, and General Forman had found a road which circled the British, and Captain Edwards had galloped along the road for a distance to see that it was clear of the enemy.[26]

Elated with the prospect, Lee was heard to say that apparently Cornwallis had no more than a strong covering party and would surely be taken. Dr. James McHenry, one of Washington's aides who was with Lee, was sent back to the commander in chief to report the good news. As related by the amiable McHenry, Lee declared "with a fixed and firm tone of voice and countenance," that Wayne would "annoy them with a few loose cannon shot" while he executed his plan of encirclement.[27]

As Lee's troops began to appear in strength on the plains below Briar's Hill, Clinton concluded that they were there to hold him back while other sections of the American army would pounce upon his baggage. More Americans, apparently militia, had been seen near Scots Meeting House on Clinton's left flank, and it was known that Morgan with his formidable riflemen was still on the right flank. The thought, too, occurred to Clinton that Washington might be trying to get to Middletown first and thus force the British to fight on unfavorable ground.[28]

Clinton accordingly ordered Colonel William Harcourt to charge Lee's vanguard with his Sixteenth Regiment of Dragoons.[29] William Harcourt, it should be remembered, was the officer who had captured Lee at Basking Ridge two years before. Son of the earl of Harcourt, he had served in the Sixteenth Regiment of Dragoons in Portugal, when Lee was his commander, and had won glory against the Spanish. In reward for capturing Lee, he was given the honor of being appointed an aide to the king. So pleased was he with his capture of Lee, that this episode of his life was the only one he ordered to be carved on his tombstone. It can then be imagined with what enthusiasm he now brought his dragoons into line for the charge. With him was the equally enthusiastic Major Banastre Tarleton, the terror of the South during months to come.

Harcourt's dragoons directed their charge against a company of American horse, probably those under Baylor. It is impossible to determine how many horsemen Lee had with his division. In all, the Americans at Monmouth may have had two or three hundred, counting those with Moylan. In any event they were weak in comparison with Clinton's formidable body of dragoons.[30]

Minutes before Harcourt charged the Americans, Lafayette sent word to the cavalry to draw back under cover of the infantry. As the American horse sped for safety, Harcourt's dragoons came thundering after them amid a cloud of dust. The charge brought the dragoons to the edge of a woods where Butler's men were waiting. Again the crack of several hundred muskets sent the dragoons racing back. As before, they had galloped right into a line of regulars formed on the hill.[31]

By this time Cornwallis's artillery had been drawn up on the hill and was answering Oswald's battery with round shot. Cannonading at a range of half a mile or so, however, had little accuracy, so that damage by either side was minor. The effect, nonetheless, was frightening enough; it could slow up an advance or delay the movement of troops. During the cannonading the Americans sustained a loss when Colonel John Durkee, covering Oswald's battery with his Connecticut and Rhode Island men, was severely wounded.

Still thinking that Clinton had only a strong covering party of perhaps two thousand men as a rear guard, Lee ordered Wayne forward with instructions to "amuse" the enemy but not press so hard as to cause Cornwallis to fall back on his reserves and spoil Lee's plan for encircling the enemy. This was asking much of Wayne, who chafed at any restraint and preferred outright assault to Lee's more subtle strategy.[32]

Within a few minutes after Butler had repulsed the dragoons and Wayne was preparing to advance, Cornwallis, acting on Clinton's order, began marching back toward Freehold. As Lee would soon find out, Cornwallis's column was no mere covering party but an entire division. The move toward Freehold with so strong a force would counteract the American drive to the left and cause Lee, Clinton hoped, to call in his flanking parties.

Cornwallis's column consisted of two battalions of the dreaded grenadiers, a battalion of light infantry, the guards, three brigades of regulars, and Hessian grenadiers in towering brass-fronted helmets. In addition, there were Harcourt's dragoons and Simcoe's Queen's Rangers and hussars. The division was a formidable fighting force which actually outnumbered the Americans by about three to two.[33]

Lord Cornwallis, second-in-command of the British forces, was an amiable gentlemen of forty, greying at the temples and of a florid complexion. After being educated at Eton, he served in Germany during the Seven Years' War as an officer of the guards, and in time inherited the title of earl. During the controversy over taxing America, he sided with the colonists, but, like the Howe brothers, he stayed in the army and served throughout the American war until his surrender at Yorktown. In the 1790's, after performing brilliantly in the campaigns in India, he entered a successful career as governor general of India.[34]

During a lull in the cannonading, much to the disgust of Lee, who thought a battlefield was no place for civilians, a party of spectators galloped along the American line. Everywhere, however, curiosity out-

weighed fear as men and boys mounted roofs and trees to view the
battle. Later in the day scores of men clung to the roof of the Tennent Meeting House to watch the course of the conflict.[35]

Surmising the meaning of Clinton's move toward Freehold and
though not giving up his plan of encirclement, Lee directed Lafayette
to take Wayne's troops and move to the right in front of the village.[36]
After ordering Lafayette to block the advance of the enemy, Lee rode
along the ravine to the place where he had stationed Scott; he intended to order Scott to commence the encircling movement. On the
way, he met both Mercer and Edwards, who reported that they had
looked all around but could not find Scott in the area where he was
supposed to be. Lee sensed that something was wrong and soon discovered that Scott had retreated to the other side of the morass, leaving Grayson stranded far up on the left. Furious because Scott had
acted without orders, Lee was at first of a mind to recall him and continue his plan to encircle the British. Still very angry when he presently met General Knox, who had ridden forward from Washington's column, Lee complained that everyone was giving orders and paying little
attention to his.[37]

Some other contingents not directly under Scott also pulled
back over the morass. Colonel Samuel Smith said he advised Colonel
Henry Jackson not to retire without orders but that he did so to get
on high defensive ground. Oswald, who had not brought his ammunition wagons over the frail bridge, said he heard men shouting, "Retreat, retreat!" Having run out of ammunition, he likewise retreated.[38]

Soon after discovering what had happened on the left flank, Lee
learned that Lafayette, pressed by Cornwallis and informed about
Scott's retreat, had fallen back to the outskirts of Freehold. He at
once abandoned all thought of trying to execute his encircling movement. Furthermore, he now admitted that the retreat, although contrary to his orders, had become absolutely necessary, since it had become too hazardous to remain beyond the third morass.[39]

Washington Irving, in his *Life of Washington*, aptly summed up
Lee's perilous situation: "Lee, instead of a mere covering party which
he had expected to cut off, had found himself front to front with the
whole rear division of the British army, and that too, on unfavorable
ground, with a deep ravine and a morass in his rear." Another nineteenth-century historian, Thomas Gordon, thought that Lee until the

last moment was determined to carry out Washington's orders at all costs. Although he perceived his mistake in assessing the size of Cornwallis's division, still he

proposed to engage on that ground, although his judgement, as was afterwards stated by himself, on an inquiry into his conduct, disapproved of it, there being a morass immediately in his rear, which could not be passed without difficulty and which would necessarily impede the arrival of reinforcements, to his aid, and embarrass his retreat should he be finally overpowered.[40]

General Clinton supported the conclusions of those historians who view Lee's position as extremely dangerous. As for Lee's support, Clinton did not think Washington could have gotten farther than the first morass, three miles from the third ravine. Clinton put it bluntly, declaring that he did not think Washington was "incautious enough to commit himself among those defiles in support of his advanced corps." In a letter to Germain, he again forcibly wrote, "had Washington been blockheaded enough to sustain Lee, I should have catched him between two defiles.[41]

Clinton furthermore pointed out that his men were comparatively fresh while Lee's, having marched six or seven miles, were all but spent. Lee testified to this when he pointed out how many had fainted and how utterly exhausted were most of the men by the time they retreated to Freehold. As Clinton also observed, he had a powerful cavalry, refreshed after a day of rest and ready to close on Lee's flanks at the first opportunity.[42] Lee, not unmindful of this fact, told McHenry near Freehold that it was all but folly to try to stand against the British with their hundreds of veteran dragoons.[43]

As Clinton advanced toward Freehold he became concerned about his flanks and decided to reinforce his corps with nearby reserves. He therefore sent word to Knyphausen to detach General James Grant with a brigade of infantry and the Seventeenth Regiment of Dragoons, to take post near Scots Meeting House near Briar's Hill. To be sure that his order did not miscarry, he sent his aide, Lieutenant Colonel Rawdon, to help Grant. But regardless of the order, Grant, who was fifty-eight and one of the oldest generals in the army, did not respond. It may be that Knyphausen, worried about his wagon train, ordered or advised Grant to remain with his own corps.[44]

While following his troops to Freehold, Lee discussed with his aides and officers the feasibility of forming a line at the village, where he had now ordered the entire division to rendezvous. Upon arriving at the town, however, he decided on reports from Lafayette and others who had been reconnoitering that it would be unwise to make a stand there. The score or more of houses which formed the village were made of wood and were too scattered to afford much protection. Furthermore, his flanks would be exposed to an encircling movement by swift-moving cavalry.[45]

After deciding against trying to hold a line at Freehold, Lee sent Brigadier General Louis Duportail to find defensible ground farther back in the direction of Washington's advancing troops. Duportail, the chief engineer for the Continental army, was then acting as one of Lee's staff officers.

Born near Orleans, Duportail was educated in a military school. As a reward for making a new set of rules for French engineers, he was admitted to the Royal Corps of Engineers as a lieutenant colonel in 1776. When Franklin arrived in Paris, Duportail was selected, with several others for the American army. After joining, just before the Battle of Germantown, he spent the winter at Valley Forge fortifying the encampment. So well was this work performed that General Howe gave it as one of his reasons for not attacking Washington. Today, Duportail is remembered as the father of the Army Corps of Engineers.

Duportail selected a line of defense running from a hill (now a Catholic cemetery) to a marsh below Carr's house. To this position, about a mile west of Freehold, Lee directed his troops.

Some of Lee's officers afterward testified that the retreat, especially from Freehold, lacked order. Scott said he saw horses trotting, with fieldpieces dragging and bouncing over the rough roads. Some officers complained that they were without orders and did not know where they were going or why they were retreating. Most of them, however, testified that they thought the retreat was as orderly as could be expected considering the heat and the necessity of keeping in the woods as much as possible for protection against the torrid sun as well as the enemy's dragoons.[46]

By this time many officers were forced to walk because their horses had given out. Colonel Brooks and Colonel Malmedy, both dismounted, were utterly exhausted by the time they got back to the first morass. Captain Stephen Olney of the Rhode Island line, one of those who testified that the retreat was as orderly as could be expected, wrote:

The heat of the day was so intense that it required the greatest efforts of the officers to keep their men in the ranks, and several of my company were so overcome and faint . . . that they said they could go no farther, but by distributing about half a pint of brandy, which I happened to have in my canteen . . . I made out to get them along.[47]

That Lee should not be blamed, as he has been, for whatever disorder occurred during the retreat is clear. He could not be everywhere, and, if disorder can be charged to anyone, it would seem to lie with the regimental officers. Some of the trouble was revealed when Major Meade brought a dispatch from Washington while Lee was at Carr's house. Meade found him astride his horse and in a bad mood. The report that Washington was still two miles away did not improve his temper. He complained to Meade that his orders had not been obeyed and that unauthorized persons had given commands. Another problem, he said, was the lack of flags to distinguish regiments and of horns for signaling.

Certainly, had the army been properly equipped with colors and horns, much needless riding in the blazing sun could have been avoided. Lee explained the seriousness of the deficiencies in his communication system:

Had not our system been so defective in these points, and the number of my Aide-de-Camps been competent, I could (such was the excellent temper of the troops) have conducted the whole of the maneuvres of this day with as much ease as ever they were performed in a common field of exercise.[48]

While at the Duportail line, American artillery exchanged shots with the British, mostly at long range and with little damage to either side. Before the retreat continued, however, some of Lee's men were charged upon by a troop of British horsemen who galloped ahead of the slow-moving troops advancing in two columns with artillery and cavalry in the center. Once again, the dragoons wheeled about and sped away after receiving a volley from the muskets of the Americans.[49]

Lee was at Carr's house for upwards of an hour before deciding that it would be unwise to try to hold the British at the line proposed by Duportail. Both armies were moving very slowly in the heat. Wayne, for instance, was nearly an hour getting from Freehold to the vicinity of Carr's house. His progress may have been slowed by his dogged reluctance to give ground or be pushed too fast by the enemy. Many regiments simply rested as long as they dared in the woods before resuming their march.

Just before leaving Carr's house, Lee talked with a local man, Captain Peter Wykoff of the Monmouth militia, who strongly advised him to make a stand on the elevation back of the first morass, where Washington later formed the main army. This was the rise, protected by a brook and a surrounding marsh, which Dickinson had occupied in the early morning. Wykoff also pointed out a higher eminence to the west, known as Comb's Hill, which was also protected by a marsh and a stream to its front. Lee, however, decided that there was no time to take advantage of this hill.[50]

Lee accepted Captain Wykoff's suggestion and sent out orders for the forming of a line on the rise beyond the bridge. The order, however, did not reach all the regimental officers, some of whom continued to retire since they did not know what was expected of them. Lee may have thought that it was not necessary for all to have the order because the whole division was headed for the bridge where they could be informed about future moves.

Washington was not within what could be called supporting distance until Lee's division had left the vicinity of Carr's house and was headed for the west morass. The center of his camp during the night before the battle was four miles west of Englishtown, and it was ten in the morning before his troops reached that village. He was then six or seven miles from Lee, who was maneuvering in front of the enemy at Briar's Hill.

Washington's division arrived at the Tennent Meeting House about one o'clock, just as Lee was leaving Carr's house, three miles away. The first inkling Washington had that there was trouble ahead came when he met a frightened young fifer who exclaimed that Lee's whole division was retreating. Washington did not entirely believe the boy and ordered him to be put under guard so that his report would not spread and cause any panic among the troops. Yet, fearing that there might be some truth in what he had heard and not having had a report from Lee for some time, he sent Lieutenant Colonel Robert Harrison and Lieutenant Colonel John Fitzgerald forward for information.[51] Harrison testified that he met in succession Grayson, William Smith, Mathias Ogden, David Rhea, and Maxwell, all of whom declared they did not know why they were retreating and were indignant over the withdrawal.[52] Here is good evidence of the fighting quality of the regimental officers, if not of their military sagacity.

The most reliable report Washington had came when he met Colonel Israel Shreve with his New Jersey troops. Shreve was not aware of Lee's plan to form on the rise behind the bridge, for he was then some distance beyond this point and was marching toward the Tennent Meeting House.[53]

After ordering Shreve to remain where he was, Washington spurred his horse forward and had just crossed the bridge and was starting up the opposite rise when he met Lee with some of his aides and subordinates.

Riding up to Lee, Washington angrily demanded the meaning of the retreat. Apparently Lee did not at first understand him. He simply said, "Sir, Sir!" On Washington's repeating the question, he apologized and attempted to explain that the nature of the ground and the superiority of the British, especially in cavalry, necessitated a retrograde action. According to General Forman, an eyewitness, Washington replied that he understood the British were but a strong covering party. Lee then said that in any event they were stronger and that prudence required a withdrawal. The sensational meeting between the two generals on the field of battle ended with Washington's remark that Lee should not have accepted the command if he had not intended to obey orders.[54]

There are many versions of this dramatic event. Eyewitnesses disagreed about details, but all admitted that Washington was enraged and that Lee seemed confused and embarrassed. Joseph Plumb Martin, who claimed that he witnessed the incident, said that Washington was "very angry." Another soldier said that Washington shouted, "My God, General Lee, What are you about?"[55]

General Scott, who saw the encounter, declared that Washington swore until the leaves trembled. Scott's own words are interesting. When asked if he ever heard Washington swear, he answered, "Yes, once, it was at Monmouth, on a day that would have made any man swear. Yes, sir, he swore on that day till the leaves shook on the trees, charming, delightfully. Never did I enjoy such swearing before or since. Sir, on that memorable day, he swore like an angel from Heaven."[56]

Scott's account, however, was given years after by an old man who probably wanted to make the affair seem as dramatic as possible. Hamilton, who was also there, maintained that Washington did not swear, although he was in a rage.[57] Another observer was Lafayette, who said, forty-six years after the episode, that Washington called Lee a "damned poltroon." Colonel Laurens, who was also there, told his father that Washington expressed astonishment at the retreat but he did not say that he had sworn or called names. Still another observer, John Brooks, simply said that Washington was very "warm" over the way things had gone.[58]

Leaving Lee perplexed and baffled, Washington rode past a hedge-row to the top of the rise. Here he met more of Lee's troops, all headed for the bridge over the Middle Spotswood Brook. The enemy, he was told, was not far behind and would soon be in sight. Realizing that something should be done to check the advance of the enemy while the main army was forming behind the brook, Washington called upon Colonel Walter Stewart, with the Third Pennsylvanians, and Lieutenant Colonel Nathaniel Ramsay, with the Third Marylanders, to take post at a point of wood on the high ground. Stewart and Ramsy, both with Wayne's brigade, responded with shouts of joy. Now they were going to get the fighting they had been eager for.

Riding back, Washington again met Lee, who was still smarting over the encounter. By this time Washington had calmed somewhat; perhaps he had given thought to the possibility that he had been too hasty. In any event, he now asked Lee if he would take command of the front line while he rode back to form the main army behind the bridge.

Shrugging off his bitterness as best he could, Lee accepted, declaring that he would do all in his power to stop the enemy and that he would be among the last to leave the field. Just then, Alexander Hamilton rode up and shouted, "I will stay here with you, dear General, and die with you, let us die here together rather than retreat." Lee looked at the young man and coolly remarked that he was as ready to die as anyone.[59]

As was his habit at a critical time or in the thick of a fight, Washington again proved himself courageous and decisive. Hamilton was unsparing in his praise: "I never saw the general to so much advantage.

His coolness and firmness were admirable. He instantly took measures for checking the enemy's advance, and giving time for the army, which was very near, to form and make proper disposition."[60]

Lafayette, naturally, was equally generous in his praise.

Never was General Washington greater in war than in this action. His presence stopped the retreat. His dispositions fixed the victory. His fine appearance on horseback, his calm carriage, roused by the animation produced by the exertion of the morning, (le dépit de la matinée) gave him the air best calculated to excite enthusiasm.[61]

Dr. James McHenry, who was with Washington, shared this admiration for the commander in chief. "The enemy," he wrote

who were advancing rapidly, elated by our retreat, were to be checked— The most advantageous ground to be siezed—The main body of the army to be formed—The enemy's intentions and dispositions to be discovered— and a new plan of attack to be concerted—and all this too in the smallest interval of time—But it is in those moments of a battle that the genius of a general is displayed, when a very inconsiderable weight determines whether it shall be a victory or a defeat.[62]

Some of this kind of praise may have been exorbitant, the encomiums of men infatuated with the memory of Washington. But it makes Lee out to be incompetent and his record shows that such was certainly not the case. He did not know that Washington's division was so close and in the absence of this knowledge his main concern was to get his men over the morass. He had already anticipated Washington by taking the precaution of covering his troops by ordering Lieutenant Colonel Jeremiah Olney, Lieutenant Colonel Henry Livingston, and Lieutenant Colonel Samuel Smith, with their respective regiments, to take position in a woods in front of the bridge.[63]

Once more in command, Lee had only a few moments to establish a line before the British appeared. Wayne, now with Stewart and Ramsay, was ordered to hold the hill at all costs to give time for the main army to form on the opposite rise.[64] Upon perceiving that Oswald, who had been firing grapeshot at the enemy, was retiring from a hillock for want of supporting infantry, Lee asked General Knox, who had stayed at the front, to direct Oswald to return to the knoll and promise support, Oswald returned immediately.. Soon Lee had Livingston's regiment stationed with the artillery, now numbering eight or ten cannon. Along a hedgerow tying the artillery on the right, with Stewart and Ramsay in the woods, Lee placed Olney with his Rhode Island and Connecticut men.[65]

Lee's line was scarcely formed before the British dragoons, headed by Harcourt, came charging; waves of grenadiers and light infantry followed. In the midst was Sir Henry Clinton himself, waving his sword and galloping "like a Newmarket jockey." Though the Americans fired volleys and poured in grapeshot, on came the enemy in waves of brilliant red.

After having fired, Olney's men charged with bayonets, pushed the enemy back, and then retired to the hedgerow. A little later, fearing that they would be outflanked, Olney and Livingston fell back toward the bridge; Oswald followed. It was during this fierce encounter that Major Simeon Thayer, second-in-command of the Rhode Islanders, lost an eye—apparently from the windage of a whizzing cannonball. Hamilton also came close to losing his life when he tumbled from his horse after it was shot. The British, likewise, had casualties. At one instant Clinton was saved only when a guard stabbed an American officer who had fired and missed.[66]

Over on the left, Stewart and Ramsay were engaged in an equally savage encounter with the enemy. So fierce was the British charge that it swept the Americans out of the woods. As the combatants emerged, all was confusion in savage hand-to-hand fighting. Although outnumbered, the Pennsylvanians fought all the way to the bridge; there Colonel Ogden and his New Jersey Blues covered the men as they crossed the causeway.[67]

On this first major clash of arms at Monmouth, casualties on either side were heavy. Colonel Stewart was carried wounded from the field and the command of his regiment fell to Lieutenant Colonel Lewis Farmer. Ramsay, battling the enemy at every step, was wounded and captured after a fierce hand-to-hand sword fight.[68]

Nathaniel Ramsay, who was thirty-four, was a brother of Dr. David Ramsay, the author of one of the first histories of the American Revolution. Both Nathaniel and David were graduates of the College of New Jersey. Nathaniel's wife was a sister of the famous artist, Charles Willson Peale, who painted Ramsay's picture during this period of his life. After his capture at Monmouth, Ramsay was a prisoner for over two years before he was finally exchanged.

While the fighting went on at the hedgerow and in the woods, Lee caught sight of a supporting regiment moving back. "Where is that damned blue regiment going?" he shouted. Colonel Henry Jackson, in command of the regiment, rode up to Lee to explain that his men were too spent to remain on the field. Lee at first paid no attention; he drew his sword and cried, "My God, you are not in command here."[69] Then he realized what Jackson was saying, put away his sword and ordered the regiment over the bridge.*

Lee's battle on the heights above the Middle Spotswood Brook lasted for nearly an hour before the pressure became so great that all were forced over the bridge. All through the engagement, Lee fought bravely while he rode from regiment to regiment to encourage the men to stand and fight. Hamilton acknowledged that he had fought valiantly and was among the last to cross the bridge and leave the field to the enemy.[70] That hour which Lee and his comrades-in-arms gave to Washington made it possible for the main division to place itself securely and prepare for the next phase of the Battle of Monmouth.

*It may well be that the "Molly Pitcher" episode took place during this encounter. Molly, whose maiden name was Mary Ludwig, had married John Casper Hayes, a barber of Carlisle, Pennsylvania, when she was about sixteen. She was reputed to have been a bright-eyed, twenty-four-year-old woman, who smoked, chewed tobacco, and swore like a trooper. During the battle, it seems, she had been carrying water when her husband, who had been manning one of the cannon, was either wounded or had fallen from exhaustion. Molly seized a ramrod and began loading and firing at the enemy.

James Sullivan Martin, who claimed to have been an eyewitness, declared that while Molly was bending over, a cannonball from the enemy's battery passed between her legs and sheared off a section of her petticoat. Embellished as the stories may be, there is a tradition that General Greene on the next day presented her to Washington, who thereupon made her a sergeant with half pay. There is no record of a federal pension ever having been given, but in 1822 Pennsylvania granted Molly Pitcher an annuity for the rest of her life because of her service at Monmouth. Martin, *Narrative,* 91-92; Thayer, *Nathanael Greene,* 248; Custis, *Recollections,* 224-25; Cook, *What Manner of Men,* 23; Salter, *Monmouth and Ocean Counties,* 221; *Proceedings of the New Jersey Historical Society,* LXX, 59; J.B. Landis, "An Investigation into the American Tradition of a Woman Known as Molly Pitcher," *Journal of American History,* V, No. 1, 83.

IV

An Unsprung Trap

While Lee was restraining the British in front of the Middle Spotswood
Brook, Washington lined up the main part of his army on the rise across
the brook. As he rested from a fall from his horse, Hamilton viewed the
troops as they marched upon the field and assumed battle formation.
Never before, Hamilton admitted, had he realized the value of military
discipline. Now he appreciated what Steuben's drilling had done. Up
until now Hamilton had not a very high opinion of the army; for good
reason it had often been called a rabble in arms. But undoubtedly it had
become, he reflected, an excellent fighting force with the capability of
battling the enemy with at least an even chance of success.[1]

Washington's main line was commanded by Major General William
Alexander, better known as Lord Stirling. Although not one of Washington's outstanding generals, Stirling was brave and dependable. After the
French and Indian War, in which he served as an aide-de-camp to General William Shirley, he went to London, where he tried unsuccessfully to
convince the House of Lords that he was entitled to an earldom.
Though unsuccessful, Alexander assumed the title and ever after was
known as Lord Stirling.

As Stirling extended his line along the rise above the Middle Spotswood Brook, each brigade marched to an appointed place. Brigadier
General Enoch Poor, a veteran of the French and Indian War known for
stopping his men periodically for prayers, was in command of the New
Hampshire troops. George Weedon, a tavern keeper at Fredericksburg,

was in charge of the Virginia troops. Jedediah Huntington, with the Connecticut troops, came from a wealthy and influential family; in 1762 his name was second on the list of graduates at Harvard. More colorful than the others was John Peter Muhlenberg, a Lutheran minister from Woodstock, Virginia. In his final sermon before joining the Continental army, his theme was taken from *Ecclesiastes,* III, i: "A time to kill, and a time to heal, a time to break down, and a time to build up." Then, when he had finished the sermon, he flung off his clerical robes and revealed his officer's uniform.

When assembled, Stirling's line, partially shielded by orchards and woods, rested solidly on the rise. One observer noted that the line was so long that it was impossible to see from one end to the other. Just below the infantry, General Knox stationed a battery of twelve cannon under the command of Lt. Colonel Edward Carrington, a Virginian who later became Greene's quartermaster in the South. Hardly had the cannon been placed for action than the battery began hurling shot at the British on the opposite hill. The British gunners returned an equally warm fire.[2]

As Lee's tired and worn-out troops staggered over the causeway spanning the brook, Washington at first stationed them near the cannon. They were not long in this position before on noticing their spent condition, he ordered Lee to take them back to Englishtown. Why he did not take Lee's advice and station them in immediate supporting distance near the Tennent Meeting House is difficult to understand. With Lee's division nearby, Washington mainfestly could have adopted a bolder course of action and perhaps have successfully outflanked the enemy.[3]

Soon after Lee arrived at Englishtown, he received an order from Washington directing him to turn his troops over to Baron von Steuben, who had charge of the reserves. Before he retired for some rest, Lee told Steuben that Washington should be on his guard since the British were capable of inflicting a severe blow.[4] After a little rest, Lee returned to the battlefield, accompanied by his aides and a retinue of faithful dogs. He intended to offer Washington his services but, before he reached the firing line, the battle was over.

During a lull in the battle following Lee's withdrawal over the bridge an incident occurred that amused Washington. Billy Lee and some other black servants had ridden to a knoll to view the enemy. Atop the height, Billy was just taking a sight on the enemy through one of Washington's field glasses when a cannonball whizzed by. Whirling about in mad haste the party came galloping back to the lines.[5]

In the morning, before commencing the march, Washington had placed Greene in command of a division. On reaching the Tennent Meeting House, Washington received messages from Knox and Hamilton advising him to send a force to the right to head off any flanking movement in that direction. He promptly ordered Greene to file off to the right with his troops and, if possible, outflank the enemy by marching to Freehold on a road skirting Comb's Hill.[6]

After marching for nearly three miles, Greene had nearly reached the Allentown road at a point about two miles from Freehold when he learned that Lee was retreating. Not knowing the strength of the British, Greene turned back so as to be able to aid Washington and Lee.[7] While his troops were retracing their steps, Greene decided to place a battery on Comb's Hill overlooking the battlefield. An order was immediately given, and soon a battery of eight or ten cannon was posted on the hill, commanded by the Chevalier Thomas Antonine Maduit Du Plessis, a man fated to be assassinated by his soldiers at Port-au-Prince following the outbreak of the French Revolution.[8]

To protect the battery Greene put six hundred men on the flanks of the cannon. The corps was commanded by Brigadier General William Woodford, a Virginian who had won fame defeating Lord Dunmore at Great Bridge at the beginning of the war. Greene posted the rest of his troops to the right of Stirling's line, thus linking Washington's division on the left with the battery on Comb's Hill. The entire line with Stirling on the left and Greene on the right resembled a great horseshoe bending around the Middle and South Spotswood brooks. It was exceptionally tight and defensible; wide flanking movements might have broken it, but such hardly seemed possible, considering the heat of the day.

After Lee had been forced over the Middle Spotswood Brook, the way was open for Clinton to launch attacks along Washington's line of battle. His first drive was apprently against Greene's troops. It is not certain at which point along the line the British made the attack. They could have marched toward the confluence of the South and Middle brooks, with the intention of crossing the streams and morass of logs and rails at a point where the marsh was not wide. If successful, this tactic could have split the American army and threatened it with destruction. More likely, Cornwallis, who led the detachment, took the less hazardous approach and sent his troops against Comb's Hill by way of Wemrock Road, approaching the hill from the south. Whichever course the British took carried them directly under the fire from the battery on the hill.

It was an awe-inspiring sight for the men on the American lines to see the enemy advancing in brilliant uniforms and with flying colors. Among them were such units as the famed Grenadier Guards, led by Sir John Wrottesly, the Cold Stream Guards, commanded by Lieutenant Colonel Henry Trelawney, and the Scots Foot Guards, with Lieutenant Colonel Cosmo Gordon at their head.[9]

As the British came in range of the battery on Comb's Hill and as they crossed open fields below the heights, cannonballs came tearing through their ranks. One shot, it was reported, knocked the muskets from the hands of a whole platoon but miraculously hurt no one. Quite understandably, the attempt on the American right collapsed as quickly as it had begun. Regardless of the intense heat, the British, after exchanging shots with some of Greene's troops, turned about and ran for the safety of woods and orchards that dotted the area. During the attack an officer was killed and Colonel Trelawney seriously wounded.[10]

Clinton's attempt to turn Stirling's flank was a far more serious maneuver than the advance on Greene's formidable position. Though subject to cannon fire from Carrington's battery, a strong corps of grenadiers and Highlanders crossed the Middle Brook several hundred yards upstream from the causeway and successfully reached an orchard after driving back the Americans. Recognizing the peril, Washington sent Colonel Joseph Cilley with nearly a thousand men, including his own New Hampshire regiment, against the enemy. With Cilley were Colonel Richard Parker with Virginians, and Colonel Alexander Scammell with the Third New Hampshire Regiment.

Joseph Cilley, a forty-four-year-old man of attractive manners, had been a New Hampshire lawyer and businessman. About Parker little is known. Scammell, a Harvard graduate, had taught school and surveyed before the war. Adjutant general for the Continental army, he had after the battle the unpleasant duty of placing General Lee under arrest.

As Cilley advanced, his men came under heavy fire from the British cannon. Fortunately the smoke of battle, which lay so thick that at times neither side could see the other, helped to screen the troops from the enemy. Through the smoke and stifling heat the Americans advanced, muskets over their shoulders, until they were within a few rods of the enemy. Then, with battle cries that resounded from the hills, they fired a volley and charged with bayonets at the tall grenadiers and the fierce-looking Black Watch Highlanders with bonnets and kilts. It was this charge, in the opinion of John Brooks, that turned the tide of battle in favor of the Americans. Soon the British were forced over the brook. Cilley did not follow but fell back to the protection of the orchard and the American battery.[11]

While Cilley was battling the enemy, Lt. Colonel Aaron Burr distinguished himself in an endeavor to outflank the British. Burr, who was only twenty-two, was leading his troops over the marsh on a flooring of logs and rails when he came under heavy fire from the British batteries. The young officer was determined to push on, thinking, perhaps rightly, that the Americans could outflank the enemy and secure a victory. Lieutenant Colonel Rudolph Bunner, who was in the lead with his Pennsylvanians, was already over the morass. The rest of Burr's men were not far behind. Just then, Lieutenant Colonel Francis Barber appeared with an order from Washington that the detachment pull back. Burr tried to argue with Barber, but the order was firm. While the troops waited, the British found their range and began pelting them with round shot. Bunner was killed and Burr's horse shot from under him. Before the corps got back to the protection of some trees, their losses were considerable. Burr blamed Washington, whom he never forgave for what he considered an act of bad generalship.[12]

While these actions were occurring to the right and left, Stirling was attacked in the center. Led by Lieutenant Colonel James Webster, the Thirty-Third Regiment and a corps of grenadiers with great impetuosity and force charged the American line near the bridge. The attack carried them farther than Clinton desired, and they were extricated from their predicament only when a strong detachment under Lieutenant Colonel William Meadows was sent to the bridge to cover their retreat. So much firing occurred during this sharp encounter that by the time the British were back, they had expended all their ammunition. As the British retreated, Washington, who constantly encouraged his men and urged them forward, was at one time within fifty feet of the enemy.[13]

Not long after the last of the British had disappeared from the vicinity of the bridge, Wayne followed the enemy with his Pennsylvanians and some Maryland and Virginia troops. He had persuaded Washington, when Lee left for Englishtown, to keep his men at the front. Craving action, he had barely placed his troops at a hedgerow stretching for several hundred feet in front of the bridge to the parsonage on the right, before he saw rows of British forming for a charge. It was the Second Battalion of Grenadiers supported by some light infantry with Lieutenant Colonel Henry Monckton at their head.

Monckton came from an influential Irish family. His brother, Robert Monckton was second-in-command under James Wolfe at the capture of Quebec in 1759. He had already proved his valor, having been wounded at Long Island and at Germantown. In addition to his courage, he had acquired a recklessness in battle, perhaps as an effect of his dissipation of a personal fortune at the gambling tables.[14]

Advancing and then dressing his men for the charge, Monckton was heard shouting, "Forward! Charge, my brave Grenadiers!" as he waved his sword and pointed at his enemy. "Steady! steady!" shouted Wayne. "Wait for the word and pick out the king birds!" As the wave of red came dashing forward, Wayne at forty paces gave the command to fire. Down went scores of the enemy, but on they came.

Colonel James Chambers, who had been wounded at Brandywine, received the brunt of the charge; soon his Pennsylvanians were locked in hand-to-hand combat with the grenadiers. Meanwhile Monckton had fallen dead near the parsonage, and a desperate struggle developed for possession of his body. In the melee, Monckton's body was seized and dragged within the American line. While this was happening, Captain William Wilson and others wrestled the colors from the grenadiers and brought the flag triumphantly back to their comrades. During the thick of the fighting, Lieutenant Colonel John Laurens nearly lost his life when his horse was shot from under him.[15]

In a matter of minutes it was all over. It was a wonderful sight, said James McHenry, to see the exalted grenadiers running back, leaving heaps of dead and wounded on the battlefield. Wayne hurriedly withdrew beyond the brook, having discovered that the enemy was about to outflank him with another corps.[16]

While the battle was raging around the parsonage, a brigade of light infantry and the Queen's Rangers with a column of horse were attempting to turn Stirling's left by a wide flanking movement. After marching up the Amboy road, past Craig's house, the British turned westward and headed toward the North Spotswood Brook, not far from the end of Washington's lines. They never came nearer. Clinton had decided that the Americans could not be routed; he recalled his flanking column.[17]

It was then about four o'clock. For the next two hours, while the infantry listened and watched with awe, the two armies engaged in a thunderous artillery duel. Judging by noise and smoke, many mistook the cannonading for the high point in the battle; in reality it was little more than an expenditure of powder and shot. Occasionally a ball hit a target, but certainly more men, especially among those serving the batteries, were laid low by the heat than by gunshot. One cannonball from the British, tradition holds, came skipping through the Tennent churchyard and killed a man sitting on a gravestone.[18]

All during the day, Brigadier General Henry Knox, a jovial and gregarious man who had operated a bookstore in Boston, did yeoman service helping Washington give commands and overseeing his batteries. Knox was one of the largest men in the American army, over six feet tall and weighing about two hundred and forty pounds. Although sometimes ridiculed for his "pompous, self-complacent walk," he was regarded as one of Washington's best generals.[19] On the British side, Knox was pitted against Brigadier General James Pattison, who with his artillerymen deserved no less praise than the Americans.

After securing his baggage by feat of arms, which he said was his primary object for attacking the Americans, Clinton discontinued the cannonading about six o'clock and pulled back beyond Carr's house. There the army had supper and rested. Washington wanted to continue the battle since he had troops with strength enough left to fight. He therefore sent General Poor with a detachment against the enemy's right, and General Woodford against the enemy's left. Night descended before either corps could contact the enemy.

Not wishing to fight Washington on the morrow since Knyphausen and his division were miles away, Clinton moved off about midnight ered that the enemy was gone, he decided not to pursue. It would be impossible, he knew, to overtake Clinton before he joined his advanced corps in the defensible hilly region around Middletown.

The Battle of Monmouth at no time approached the proportions of a general battle. It was a battle of detachments; the action shifted from place to place. Nevertheless, it was hard-fought and bloody. No doubt Washington's army performed better than on any previous or later occasion. Indeed, at no other time during the war did Washington have the pleasure of seeing his soldiers chase the grenadiers from the field of battle. As John Watts De Peyster wrote, this was the first time that the American army demonstrated the skill and maneuverability of a fighting machine.[20]

Even the British admitted that Washington at last had an army not to be despised. The rebels, wrote Andrew Bell in his diary, stood better than ever before. Some British officers still scoffed at their opponents, but the large majority seemed to agree that the Americans had retreated in good order and had fought well in what they referred to as skirmishes.[21]

American opinion naturally was much more enthusiastic than the British. James McHenry summarized the battle thus: "Although the victory was not so extensive as we could wish, yet it has every substantial and unequivocal proof of its being one. We gained the field of battle before evening—We camped on the ground that night."[22] Hamilton was of like mind. He wrote to Elias Boudinot: "You know my way of thinking about our army, and that I am not about to flatter it. I assure you I never was pleased with them before this day."[23]

After the battle, in general orders Washington congratulated the army for the victory over "the flower of the British Troops." The militia, too, came in for praise: Washington thanked them "for their noble Spirit" in opposing the enemy and making it possible for the Continental army to catch up and engage the enemy.[24]

For Washington's generalship at Monmouth, there was criticism from the start. That he held his division too far back to be in supporting distance should Lee get into trouble did not go unnoticed. Lee, besides censuring Washington for sending his division back to Englishtown, said that the British should have been permitted to cross the bridge in force; they could then have been crushed between sections of the American army. Lee's strictures have been repeated by some historians, the first of whom was Edward Langworthy, who wrote a biography of Lee within about a decade after his death.

Contrary to Lee's thinking, it is unlikely that Clinton could have been enticed over the brook in greater force if Washington had shown the appearance of weakness. But Washington could, it seems, have allowed Webster's troops to plunge deeper within his lines and then cut them off and captured the corps. Instead Washington brought pressure to bear upon the British vanguard when it rushed over the bridge. Clinton saw the danger they were in and not only called them back but expressed his displeasure over their impetuousness. Their enthusiasm, he declared, carried them much farther than prudence warranted.[25]

That Washington did not attempt to lure the British into a trap beyond the bridge or to send out flanking columns after the enemy had fallen back was predictable given the cautious and conservative nature of his generalship. All through the battle he remained securely posted behind the brook and morass and made no attempt to outflank the enemy or bring on a more general engagement. The detachments of Cilley and Wayne never advanced far beyond the brook. Cilley was sent out to drive back a British corps threatening the main line. Only Wayne's advance could be considered an offensive, but that was conducted with but a few hundred men. In the light of his own cautious behavior, Washington's censure of Lee may appear paradoxical.

Before the main army reached the field of battle, Washington, it is true, had ordered Greene to circle Comb's Hill and fall on the enemy's flank near Freehold. Judge William Johnson, in his life of Greene, wrote that in reality, for retiring without orders, Greene was more censurable than Lee, whose orders were discretionary. After Greene had retired to support the main army, Washington, not knowing the strength of the enemy or how well his lines would hold, no doubt was justified in keeping Greene for his right wing. But he could have sent detachments to outflank the enemy after the British had pulled back from the bridge and were no longer a threat to his line.[26]

A perplexing question arises as to why both Washington and Greene failed to order Morgan to bring his corps into action. As directed by Washington on the night before the battle, Lee had ordered Morgan to be ready to attack. However, at twelve-thirty, when Lee was retreating near Freehold, Washington sent Morgan a note which read:

I have just received your Letter by the Dragoon; as your Corps is out of supporting Distance I would have you confine yourself to observing the motions of the Enemy, unless an opportunity offers of intercepting some small Parties; and by no means to come to an Engagement with your whole Body unless you are tempted by some very evident advantage.[27]

Washington's order appears singular when it is considered that all during the day Morgan was but three miles south of Freehold and eager for battle. He could easily have joined Lee at Freehold or Briar's Hill or have come to the aid of Greene had the latter marched to Freehold. At about eleven in the morning, he sent out a rider who found Wayne near Freehold. Asked what Morgan should do, Wayne sarcastically answered that he could decide for himself since Lee was retreating.[28]

Daniel Morgan was a fighter; to have to lie idle at Richmond's Mill while the cannons were thundering must have been most galling to so hardened a warrior. Now forty-one, he had been with Braddock as a wagoner during the fateful campaign that opened the French and Indian War. In that war, because he struck a British officer, he received several hundred lashes before he fainted. Afterward the officer apologized for being in the wrong, and the good-hearted Morgan forgave him. When the Revolution began, he organized a regiment of sharpshooters from the frontier and gained fame at Saratoga by turning the tide of battle. He is best remembered for his astonishing victory over Tarleton at Cowpens, in 1781, when the British detachment was all but annihilated.[29]

If Greene had circled the British and come in behind the enemy near Freehold, Washington might have won a victory which could have ended the war. Accompanied by Morgan with his six-hundred riflemen, he could have attacked the enemy's rear while Washington pressed forward with Stirling's troops. Washington also could have strengthened his flanks if he had had Moylan's horse with the army instead of engaged in a useless endeavor to impede Knyphausen's march. Near Freehold, Greene would have encountered the Hessian grenadiers, who presumably would have offered little resistance, having refused to join in the battle: the day, they said, was too hot for fighting. After Cornwallis had been crushed, the remainder of Clinton's army under Knyphausen no doubt could have been headed off and forced to surrender. But all of this is only speculation. Washington's and not Lee's caution and reluctance to take chances precluded the possibility of reaping a great victory.

During the day, men on both sides apparently worried more about the heat and thirst than about the bullets of the enemy. As Captain Stephen Olney wrote: "Suffering and distress from the heat on that day, were greater than the fear of death from our foes." At one time nearly a whole line of grenadiers collapsed from the heat and fell helplessly as they were attempting to charge up a rise. Tongues were so

swollen and throats so parched that many men were unable to speak.
One soldier told of soldiers dying on the spot from drinking too much
cold water when they found a spring or brook. Sometimes soldiers
from both sides lay sprawled not far from one another at a brook as
they sought to quench their thirst.

Of those who died, a surprisingly large number succumbed from
sheer heat and exhaustion. During the hottest part of the day, the tem-
perature soared to nearly one hudred degrees, and the air was humid
and heavy with smoke. More British than Americans died from the heat
since they carried heavy packs and were clothed in woolen. In addition,
the British were more often on the offensive. In contrast, the Americans took off their coats during the marching and fighting and were often seen stripped to the waist.[30]

Losses for the British were somewhat higher than for the Americans. Clinton put his dead at one hundred and twenty-four, with fifty-
nine dead from heat exhaustion. This is undoubtedly too low a figure,
since the Americans reported that they had buried over two hundred of
the enemy. Clinton thanked Washington for the honorable burial of
Henry Monckton, who was interred in the graveyard at the Tennent
Meeting House. A stone still marks the place where the brave officer
was buried. Clinton estimated the number of his wounded at one hundred and seventy. Another sixty-four were missing and presumably dead
or deserted. When the British marched away, they left doctors behind
to help the wounded on both sides. Many of the wounded were taken
to the Episcopal church in Freehold, which was used as a field hospital.[31]

Most American sources place the Continental losses at about sixty
killed and one hundred and fifty wounded. These figures undoubtedly
are too low, although the much higher British estimates of American
losses are exaggerations. Besides Lieutenant Colonel Bunner of the Pennsylvania line and Major Edward B. Dickinson of the Virginia forces,
six other commissioned officers were killed. Altogether about twenty-
six officers (the surprisingly large number reflects their valor) were
wounded. Among those wounded with the rank of colonel or lieutenant
colonel were Henry Beekman Livingston, Walter Stewart, John Laurens,
John Durkee, Francis Barber, and John Fitzgerald.[32]

After resting his men, Clinton stole away by moonlight and joined
his advance corps some time the following day. Since the moon set at
ten fifty-five that night, it has been noted that most, if not all, of the

march was performed in pitch dark. John Trumbull in *McFingal* satirized Clinton's escape from Washington's army.

> He forms his camp with great parade,
> While evening spreads the world in shade,
> Then still, like some endangered spark,
> Steals off on tiptoe in the dark,
> Yet writes his king in boosting tone,
> How grand he marched by light of moon.

It took two days for Clinton to get to Sandy Hook. Another five days passed as he waited for transports. While he was marching to Sandy Hook, Morgan and Moylan kept as close to the enemy as possible. It must have been with a sigh of relief that Clinton sailed for New York on July 5. Clinton's retreat through New Jersey, however, has been considered by military men as a masterpiece in generalship. Baron Von Ochs, an early nineteenth century military critic, declared that his march was "more remarkable than that of Moreau through the Black Forest in 1796."[33]

Only a few days after the British left New Jersey, a French fleet commanded by Comte Charles Henri Théodat d'Estaing arrived off the Hook with twelve ships of the line and three frigates manned by eleven thousand sailors and marines. British authorities admitted that there could have been another Saratoga at Sandy Hook had the French arrived a few days earlier, since Lord Howe's fleet was not nearly as strong as the French. "Our retreat," wrote Clinton, "was critical as d'Estaing arrived off the Hook three days after it was completed."[34] Furthermore, Clinton knew that he left the Hook with only one day's supply of provisions.

During the evening following the Battle of Monmouth there was much talk in Washington's camp about all that had happened. Conversation especially turned upon every aspect of Lee's retreat from Briar's Hill, since Washington's reprimand on the field was soon known throughout the army. Some condemned Lee, others were not sure how to explain the retreat, while a large number felt that the action was justified considering the circumstances. Some of those who blamed Lee and thought that he had defaulted on a chance of giving the enemy a resounding defeat were Wayne, Hamilton, Laurens, Scott, and Mathias Ogden. Lee's warmest friends and supporters were his aides and lieutenants. Most of the generals, too, although all the circumstances of the retreat were not known, saw the necessity of the retreat and did not blame Lee. Nevertheless, criticism reached Lee's ears and angered him. He thought that Washington should have acknowledged his mistake and apologized for upbraiding him on the field of battle.

By the time the officers had ended their talk and settled down for the night, most of the soldiers were sound asleep. Washington slept on the ground under an apple tree, where he shared a cloak with Lafayette.[35] At Englishtown, Lee spent a restless and fitful night with thoughts of his treatment by Washington tormenting his mind.

V

Appeal to a "Candid World"

Two days after the Battle of Monmouth, Lee sent Washington (who had not mentioned his name in an order congratulating the army for its performance at Monmouth), a letter asking for an explanation of the encounter on the field of battle. Written from Englishtown, the letter read:

From the knowledge I have of your Excellency's character, I must conclude, that nothing but misinformation of some very stupid, or misrepresentation of some very wicked persons, could have occasioned your making use of such very singular expressions as you did, on my coming up to the ground where you had taken post; they imply'd, that I was guilty of either disobedience of orders, of want of conduct, or want of courage. Your Excellency will therefore infinitely oblige me, by letting me know, on which of these three articles you ground your charge, that I may prepare for my justification; which I have the happiness to be confident I can do, to the Army, to the Congress, to America, and to the World in general.

So far, unless one were particularly sensitive, there was little in the letter which could be considered offensive.

Lee continued:

Your Excellency must give me leave to observe, that neither yourself, nor those about your person, cou'd from your situation, be in the least judges of the merits or demerits of our manoeuvres; and, to speak with

a becoming pride, I can assert, that to these manoeuvers the success of
the day was entirely owing. I can boldly say, that had we remained on
the first ground, or had we advanc'd, or had the retreat been conducted
in a manner different from what it was, this whole army, and the interest of America, would have risk'd being sacrificed.

Although many historians have agreed with Lee that his action probably
saved the army from disaster, it was doubtlessly improper for him to
have made this declaration in terms so bold and boastful.

But it was the next few lines which must have angered Washington
and caused him to order a trial by court-martial rather than endeavor to
smooth Lee's ruffled feathers. Lee wrote:

I ever had (and I hope ever shall have), the greatest respect and veneration for General Washington; I think him endow'd with many great and
good qualities; but in this instance, I must pronounce, that he has been
guilty of an act of cruel injustice towards a man who certainly has some
pretensions to the regard of ev'ry servant of this country; and, I think,
Sir, I have a right to demand some reparation for the injury committed;
and unless I obtain it, I must, in justice to myself, when this campaign
is closed (which I believe will close the war), retire from a service, at
the head of which is placed a man capable of offering such injuries.

Lee softened the barbs in the last remark by adding:

But, at this same time, in justice to you, I must repeat that I from my
soul believe, that it was not a motion of your own breast, but instigated
by some of those dirty earwigs who will for ever insinuate themselves
near persons in high office; for I am really convinced, that when General Washington acts from himself, no man in his army will have reason
to complain of injustice or indecorum.[1]

Washington's answer was written on June 30, the day he received
Lee's letter. "I have received your letter (dated, through mistake, the
1st of July)," wrote Washington, "expressed, as I conceive, in terms
highly improper." After making it clear that he found Lee's letter offensive, he commented on his encounter with Lee on the battlefield:

I am not conscious of having made use of any very singular expressions
at the time of my meeting you, as you intimate. What I recollect to
have said, was dictated by duty, and warranted by the occasion. As
soon as the circumstances will permit, you shall have an opportunity

either of justifying yourself to the army, to Congress, to America, and to the world in general; or convincing them that you were guilty of a breach of orders, and of misbehaviour before the enemy, on the 28th inst., in not attacking them as you had been directed, and in making an unnecessary, disorderly, and shameful retreat.[2]

Later, at the court-martial, Lee explained how he had waited for an apology from Washington before writing to him:

I must beg leave, likewise, to observe to the Court, that from the time this, as to me it appear'd, cruel injustice was done me, to the time I wrote the first letter, was an interval I believe of more than forty hours; during which I waited in sanguine hopes that His Excellency would be better informed of facts, and that the instant he was undeceiv'd, he would make me some apology for the mistake lain under.

But instead of an apology Lee received notice from Washington that he would be tried for misconduct at Monmouth. He told of his reaction in these words:

But when, instead of the apology I had flattered myself with, these thundering charges were brought against me, comprehending the blackest military crimes of the whole black catalogue, I was more than confounded, I was thrown into a stupor, my whole faculties were for a time benumm'd; I read and read it over a dozen times, and thought it still a delusion, but when I wak'd and was convinc'd of the reality, I sat and wrote the second letter, which it seems constitutes a part of my criminality.[3]

In the second letter, Lee, whose anger must have been rising by the hour, sarcastically and insultingly wrote:

You cannot afford me greater pleasure than in giving me the opportunity of showing to America, the sufficiency of her respective servants, I trust, that the temporary power of office, and the tinsel dignity attending it, will not be able, by all the mists they can raise, to offiscate [obfuscate] the bright rays of truth.[4]

Lee then sent a third letter which read in part:

I have reflected on both your situation and mine; and beg leave to observe, that it will be for our mutual convenience, that a Court of Enquiry should be immediately ordered; but I could wish it might be a Court Martial: for, if the affair is drawn into length, it may be difficult to collect the necessary evidences, and perhaps bring on a paper war betwixt the adherents of both parties, which may occasion some disagreeable feuds on the Continent; for all are not my friends, nor all your admirers.[5]

Washington complied with Lee's request for a court-martial, but the trial did not preclude the eruption of a "paper war."

On the day that the exchange of letters took place, Wayne and Scott sent Washington a letter in which they severely criticized Lee's generalship at Monmouth. Whether or not this letter reached Washington before he wrote Lee and had a bearing upon his answer is not known. But in any event Washington must have already heard what these officers thought of the retreat. Most likely they had already seen Washington and informed him of their views, and the letter was simply to make it official. The two officers declared: "Thus were these several select detachments unaccountably drawn off without being suffered to come to action, although we had the most pleasing prospect from our numbers and position, of obtaining the most glorious and decisive victory." In conclusion they stated:

We have taken the liberty of stating these facts, in order to convince the world that our retreat from the Court House was not occasioned by the want of numbers, position, or wishes of both officers and men to maintain that post. We also beg leave to mention, that no plan of attack was ever communicated to us, or notice of a retreat, until it had taken place in our rear, as we suppos'd by General Lee's orders.[6]

On July 1, Washington made his report to Congress on the Battle of Monmouth. When he came to the point of Lee's retreat, the commander in chief wrote: "After marching about five Miles, to my great surprise and mortification, I met the whole advanced Corps retreating, and, as I was told, by General Lee's orders, without having made any opposition, except one fire given by a party under the command of Col. Butler, on their being charged by the Enemy's Cavalry, who were repulsed." Then Washington described how the line was formed which checked the enemy's advance until Stirling had time to form his troops on the rise behind the west morass. In describing this action, however, he did not mention that Lee took over the command again and valiantly led the troops in their desperate struggle with the enemy. As Washington described it in his letter:

I proceeded immediately to the Rear of the Corps, which I found closely pressed by the Enemy, and gave directions for forming part of the retreating troops, who by the brave and spirited conduct of the Officers, and aided by some pieces of well served Artillery, checked the Enemy's advance, and gave time to make a disposition of the left wing and second line of the Army upon an eminence, and in a wood a little in the Rear covered by a morass in front.[7]

The charges brought against Lee as set forth in the judge advocate's bill to the court were on three counts, reflecting as they did what Washington had said in his letter of June 28. First he was charged "for disobedience of orders, in not attacking the enemy on the 28th of June, agreeable to repeated instructions." The second charge was "for misbehavior before the enemy on the same day, by making an unnecessary, disorderly, and shameful retreat." Lastly he was charged with "disrespect to the Commander-in-Chief in the two letters dated the 1st of July and the 28th of June.[8] These charges were delivered to Lee when Alexander Scammell, the adjutant general, informed Lee that he was under arrest.

When Lee read the charges against him he must have been furious. In a letter to Robert Morris, with whom he had always been on good terms, Lee used some of his most virulent invectives. "To use the words of my Lord Chatham," wrote Lee, "have we not a gracious Prince [Washington] on the Throne? Is he not still the same? I trust he is; but there is something rotten betwixt him and his people – not content with robbing me and the brave men under my command of the honor due to us – a most hellish plan has been formed (and I may say at least not discourag'd by Head Quarters) to destroy forever my honour and reputation." Then after describing how he had saved the army from disaster, he concluded:

The General has the madness to charge me with making a shameful retreat–I never retreated in fact (for 'till I joined him it was not a retreat but a necessary and I may say in my own defence masterly manoeuvre). I say I never retreated but by his positive order who invidiously sent me out of the field when victory was assur'd. Such is my recompense for having sacrificed my Friends, my connexions, and perhaps my fortune for having twice extricated this man and his whole army out of perdition, and now having given him the only victory he ever tasted.[9]

On the day he wrote to Robert Morris, Lee sent a similar letter to Isaac Collins, editor of the *New Jersey Gazette.* He explained that the reason for his letter was a "most invidious, dishonest, and false relation" of the battle which had appeared in the last issue of the *Gazette.* As a corrective, Lee gave Collins what amounted to a very good summary of what happened. He wrote: "To call the affair a complete victory would be a dishonorable gasconade. It was indeed a very handsome check, which did the Americans honor." With this introduction he proceeded to defend what he called his "retrograde action" to the west morass where he met the main army. As to the battle as a whole, he said, "It was difficult to say which was the decisive point - it was a battle in pieces, and by dint of fighting in a variety of places - in the plain and in the woods - by advancing and retreating, the enemy were at last worn down."[10] This letter was printed in the next issue of the *New Jersey Gazette.*

The letter earlier printed in the *New Jersey Gazette* which gave offense to Lee was written by Joseph Reed, with whom he had always been on friendly terms. Reed's report on Lee's part in the battle was not derogatory or offensive, but it omitted any reference to Lee's praiseworthy defense of the line in front of the west morass. Regarding the advance, Reed's account read: "About half a mile beyond the Court House, General Lee began his attack, and drove the enemy for some time; when they being reinforced, he was obliged to retreat in turn, 'till met by General Washington with the main army, which formed on the first advantageous ground." The admission that the retreat was forced must have pleased Lee. However, he must have been far from pleased when he read on and found that Reed gave Washington all the credit for the victory. "Our success," he wrote, ". . . is to be wholly ascribed to the good disposition made by his Excellency, supported by the firmness and bravery of both officers and men."[11]

That Washington did not bring charges before Lee wrote to him suggests that he intended to let the matter drop. Over a century ago the historian Thomas Gordon wrote: "General Washington had taken no measures in consequence of the events of the day, and probably, would have come to no resolution, concerning them, . . . had he not received from Lee a letter, in very unbecoming terms. . . ." Had Lee explained himself rather than been intemperate, Gordon believed, no public examination of the question would have occurred.[12] Gordon's analysis, however, overlooks the fact that Wayne and Scott submitted a formal complaint against Lee on July 2, the day on which Washington informed Lee that he would be tried for his conduct during the battle.[13]

There also can be little doubt that if Washington showed Lee's letters to Hamilton, the latter would have recommended bringing strong charges against Lee. Hamilton entertained deep suspicions of Lee. As early as July 5, he wrote to Elias Boudinot, "This man is either a driveler in the business of soldiership or something much worse."[14] Years later in a eulogy to Greene, he compared the latter's stand at Springfield with Lee's conduct at Monmouth. "Here let me recall to your indignant view," he exclaimed, "the flower of the American infantry flying before an enemy that scarce dared to pursue—vanquished without a blow—vanquished by their obedience to the command of a leader who meditated their disgrace."[15] The eminent historian Sydney George Fisher observed that Hamilton was apparently the source of the suspicion that Lee's conduct at Monmouth was treacherous. Hamilton, he thought, convinced Boudinot and John Laurens that such was a fact and thus caused the rumor to spread.[16]

John Laurens wrote to his father on July 2 that he thought Clinton's whole army would have been destroyed "but for a defect of abilities or good will of the commanding officer of our advanced corps." In his answer, the father spoke of the "Snare" from which Washington had escaped. Part of the letter is obliterated, but it is plain that his reference to "a concerted Plan by which our Army was to have been disgraced, perhaps ruined" refers to Lee.[17] One does not have to rely on imagination to appreciate how suspicion was magnifying and spread at a great pace. Captain William Watson of the Massachusetts line wrote that the story of Lee's disobedience had spread far and wide.[18]

Some writers have given credence to a story related by George Washington Parke Custis. It concerns Dr. David Griffith, a chaplain with the Virginia troops, who, reportedly, went to Washington on the night before the battle and advised him to beware of Lee, whom he suspected of plotting treason. Custis obtained his information from Lieutenant Colonel George Nicholas—who was not at the battle, having resigned from the army the year before. The story, hearsay and gossip, was related by Custis long years after the event. Significantly, in a letter to his wife written two days before the battle, Dr. Griffith did not mention any suspicion of Lee.[19]

In spite of rampant suspicions regarding Lee's conduct, many officers hesitated to jump at hasty conclusions. McHenry, who was a very good friend of Washington's, wrote that he could not understand the reason for the retreat but that he would withhold judgment until the affair was clarified. Dr. William Shippen, chief of the medical division, wrote his brother-in-law, Richard Henry Lee, that in effect there were actually many officers in camp who supported Lee's action at Monmouth. Generals, in fact, who could understand tactical reasons better than field officers, were inclined to support Lee.[20] Enemy officers, as already noted, were unanimously of the opinion that he had acted correctly. Clinton's words, it will be remembered, were very telling:

For I could not entertain so bad an opinion of Mr. Washington's military abilities, as to suppose he would risk his *avant garde* over those difficult passes without the support of his army, or that he would even venture to support through such a country.[21]

For the distasteful assignment of serving on the court to try Lee, Lord Stirling was chosen to be president. The others were generals Smallwood, Poor, Woodford, and Huntington and eight colonels. None of the officers chosen had been with Lee's command during the battle. The witnesses, of course, would be those who had been with Lee and had seen what had transpired during the day. John Lawrence, the judge advocate general, was in charge of presenting the case against Lee.

General Scott, followed by Wayne, was the first to testify. They asserted that Lee had orders to "attack the enemy on their march, at all events, and that General Washington would be near us to support us with the main army." Wayne also declared that he believed Washington desired a general battle with the enemy.[22] On the stand, Meade concurred with Wayne that Washington was "anxious to bring on a general engagement between the two armies."[23]

Mercer and Oswald, among others, gave strong testimony in favor of Lee. Regarding the first drawback at Briar's Hill, Lee cross-examined John Brooks, asking him, "Did you hear me express great indignation at General Scott's quitting the ground?" "I did repeatedly," answered Brooks. To reinforce his testimony, Brooks declared,

Upon my first coming up with you, some distance this side of the Court-House, after the retreat began, you informed me that several battalions had retired without your knowledge, and contrary to your orders, but

observed, although it was extremely unsoldierly, yet you believed it to
be a very happy thing for the army, as the enemy were so much superior
both in infantry and cavalry, in cavalry especially; for had that not been
the case, that whole detachment at least must have been sacrificed, or
words to that effect.

As to the maintenance of order while retreating, Brooks said: "The retreat from the Court-House to Carr's House was performed, as far as I
saw it, with great deliberation and in good order."[24]

General Knox was another witness whose testimony bore much
weight. He admitted that the ground favored the British all during Lee's
retreat. During the proceedings, Lee asked Knox: "Did I observe to
you how unluckily the eminences were situated through the country,
that those near the enemy regularly commanded those near us?" "I
recollect the circumstances," answered Knox, who from all appearances
had no relish for the proceedings.[25]

On the other hand, Wayne, who had denounced Lee's retreat so
vehemently did not waver in his opinion in the face of evidence to the
contrary. In a letter to Light-Horse Harry Lee, he said that Lee "is now
in Arrest & from present Appearances will not Continue long in the Service—a note from him to a Mr. Collins, printer of the Jersey paper—
Savours of Insanity or flows from a *Worse Cause.*"[26]

As the testimony unfolded, notwithstanding contradictory evidence, a fairly clear picture appeared as to what happened at Monmouth.
But notwithstanding all the evidence pointing to Lee's reasons for retreating, the court reached a decision on August 12. It found him guilty
on all three charges. The second charge, that he had made "an unnecessary, disorderly, and shameful retreat," was softened; the word "shameful" was deleted. Having reached a verdict, the court suspended Lee
from the army for one year.[27]

That the decision of the court was a travesty of justice seems un-
questionable. The decision was reached in the face of a body of evidence
which showed that Lee's orders from Washington were discretionary and
that in the opinion of many observers the retreat was justified and generally not disorderly. As Lee said, "I manoeuvered my antoagonists from
their advantageous ground into as disadvantageous a one . . . without
losing a single gun, a single color, or sacrificing a single Battalion," during the long and grueling retreat of nearly three miles.[28] Years later,
Lee wrote to Greene:

I have long wish'd to thank you my Dr [Dear] Sir, likewise for the handsome, and generous part you have acted by me. My friends Edwards and [Light-Horse] Harry Lee have frequently inform'd me, of the generous indignation you have express'd at the unworthy and scoundrel treatment I have receiv'd.[29]

From the time of the verdict until now, it has been argued that Lee's sentence was too light if he was indeed guilty as charged. On the other hand, if he was not guilty, the verdict was a miscarriage of justice. The fact that the sentence called for suspension from the army for only one year suggests that the court itself realized that the grounds for convicting Lee (except for the charge of using disrespectful language toward Washington) were very tenuous. That the decision was a partisan one, that Lee was sacrificed to save Washington from embarrassment and an implied lack of confidence in his generalship appear to be undeniable. No doubt Lee's intemperate utterances had an important bearing on the way the court voted on all the charges.

Prior to the verdict, Lee had written Reed that he recoiled from the thought of using his friends to gain support throughout the country. "I ask only for common justice," he told Reed. Then he added bitterly,

No attack it seems can be made on General Washington, but it must recoil on the assailant—I have ever honour'd and respected him as a Man and as a Citizen—but if the Circle which surround him chuse to erect him as an infallible Divinity, I shall certainly prove a Heretick.[30]

Of all Lee's friends, none was more disturbed by the decision of the court than Major Evan Edwards. "I am shock'd confounded, and exceedingly chagrin'd to hear the Court have adjudged you guilty of all Charges aledg'd against you," he wrote to Lee. That the decision, however, was in line with public opinion was amply evident. Edwards added that so great was the feeling against Lee in Philadelphia that he almost was mobbed while defending him.[31]

The next scene of the drama was enacted in Philadelphia, where the Continental Congress undertook to review the case and to decide whether to acquit Lee or uphold the decision of the court. In reality, the result was well-nigh a foregone conclusion, since a vote to vacate the decision of the court would have been tantamount to an expression of lack of confidence in the commander in chief.

For a while, however, many of those keenly watching the flow of sentiment in Philadelphia were not at all sure that the decision of the court would be upheld. From the beginning, Congress divided sharply along the lines of the Conway Cabal of the previous winter when Washington was under fire. Among the most prominent congressmen who took Lee's side were Samuel Adams, James Lovell, Thomas Burke, and Richard Henry Lee, all of whom had been critics of Washington during the preceding winter. Hearing what was happening in Congress, John Laurens wrote to Hamilton that General Lee had "leaguered himself with the old faction and gained many sympathizers."[32]

Congress opened the hearings on Lee's trial by ordering one hundred copies of the court-martial proceedings to be printed for the use of the members. Then it did nothing until September, when it decided not to consider additional evidence submitted by Lee. He had persuaded Major John Clark to answer some questions about the battle. Clark thought that the request should have been made during the trial but said it would be "cruel" to withhold information. In his statement, he declared that he delivered an order from Washington to Lee during his advance on Briar's Hill which in his opinion was "discretionary" in nature. He also said that Lee asked him to tell Washington that he was retreating under necessity. Congress refused to accept this piece of evidence and ordered the papers returned to Lee.[33]

At this time, however, many in Congress thought that Lee's case was far from lost. According to Colonel Walter Stewart, Richard Henry Lee was doing all in his power to make the people believe "that General Lee was the Salvation of our army at Monmouth."[34] Gouverneur Morris told Washington that Lee's fate was hanging "by the Eye Lids" with Congress divided on how to proceed in the matter.[35]

Early in December the *Pennsylvania Packet* printed an article by Lee which he called his vindication to the public. In it Lee presented a good defense of his actions at Monmouth. Nothing new was disclosed. "A thousand wicked and low artifices, during my trial, were used to render me unpopular," he exclaimed. Continuing, he wrote:

One of the principal was to throw out that I had endeavoured, on every occasion to depreciate the American valor, and the character of their troops. There never was a more impudent falsehood . . . [for he ever] had the highest opinion of the courage and other good qualities of the Americans as soldiers.[36]

This was indeed true.

When Congress finally dealt with Lee's case, William Drayton of South Carolina moved to consider the charges all together. William Paca of Maryland opposed this move and insisted on having the charges considered separately. Drayton won out, and all three charges were voted on together.[37]

The verdict was reached on December 5, when Congress, voting by states, cast six votes for upholding the court and two for Lee. Massachusetts and Georgia voted for Lee's acquittal. Delaware abstained, while Virginia, New Jersey, Maryland, and New Hampshire lost their votes because their members were equally divided on the issue or were missing at the roll call. This left Connecticut, Rhode Island, New York, Pennsylvania, and North and South Carolina upholding the decision of the court. In all, sixteen congressmen voted against Lee and seven for him.[38]

Probably most of the delegates who stayed away felt that Lee was innocent of the charges against his military conduct, but they were not willing to repudiate Washington. The strongest support came from Massachusetts, with Samuel Adams and James Lovell making the vote two out of three in favor of Lee. Richard Henry Lee, one of Lee's strongest supporters, had his vote negated when the only other Virginian present voted against Lee.[39]

After the verdict was delivered, James Rivington reflected British opinion when he wrote in his *Royal Gazette* that all the world knew that Lee had saved the American army at Monmouth and that the decision was purely a partisan vote to save Washington from embarrassment.[40]

Sentiment like that was not confined to the British side. Francois Louis de Fleury, a lieutenant colonel in the American corps of engineers, told Major Edwards that it was "everywhere known in France" that Lee had been "ill treated."[41] Benjamin Rush, the Philadelphia physician who "blushed" for the conscience of his fellow congressmen, wrote: "Lee is innocent of the charges brought against him, he saved our Army, & country on the 28th of June." But, he concluded, to have reversed the decision of the court "would impeach the veracity and conduct of our commander-in-chief, & he possesses nearly as much influence over the resolutions of our Congress as the King of Britain does over the Acts of the British Parliament."[42] Dr. James Thacher, surgeon for the Continental army, called the decision a "mortal wound" to a lofty spirit,[43] and Light-Horse Harry Lee declared "the records of the court-martial manifest in their face the error of the sentence."[44]

Not long after, Lee was challenged to a duel by John Laurens for speaking and writing disrespectfully about Washington. Lee was not the only one spreading these stories, some of which were very slanderous. Washington, it was said, was mean to his servants and was positively immoral.[45] Lee accepted the challenge and informed Laurens that he would duel with pistols the following day.[46] Lee was up to his usual form, sarcastically observing that it seemed odd that one gentlemen should fight a battle belonging to another. "However," he told Laurens, "if he wished to revive the medieval custom whereby any knight might be called to serve as a champion for old women, widows, and priests," he was willing to oblige him.[47]

Lee and his second, Major Edwards, arrived ahead of the others at the designated spot outside of Philadelphia. Edwards, always talkative, entertained Lee with "metaphysical subleties on predestination, free will, etc., a little in the style of the Brissotins in a future state, when on their way to the guillotine," Alexander Graydon recalled. Presently Laurens appeared with his second, Alexander Hamilton, and Lee proposed that they advance and fire when they pleased. Laurens agreed. At the signal the combatants advanced to within fifteen feet of each other. Both fired at about the same time, and Laurens's ball wounded Lee in the side. McHenry, who was also there, thought that Lee did not fire but heard him say to Laurens, "You may fire at me all day Sir if it will amuse you; what I have said I am not disposed to recall."

Since each had two pistols, Laurens was preparing for a second shot when the seconds discovered that Lee was wounded. At once all went to help the wounded man who said that it was but a trifle and that Laurens should have his second shot. Both seconds refused, and the duel ended. Lee showed no animosity toward Laurens, whom he barely knew. Afterward, he declared that "The young fellow behaved splendidly, I could have hugged him."[48]

By this time it appeared as though Lee might become involved in a succession of duels. Just before the duel with Laurens, Baron von Steuben sent him a challenge because of caustic remarks he had made about the Baron's conduct at Monmouth. He had referred to Steuben as a "distant spectator" of most of the events of the day. The incident closed when Lee wisely declined to duel with the baron, after assuring him that he had no intention of questioning his valor or courage.[49]

With William Henry Drayton of South Carolina who had been one of Lee's bitter foes in Congress, Lee was not so indulgent. In March, he challenged Drayton to a duel for asserting, among other things, that Lee was publicly disgraced. Lee was bitterly vituperative. "I find that you are as malignant a Scoundrel," he wrote, "as you are universally allow'd to be a ridiculous and disgusting Coxcomb." He agreed with a remark of Drayton's that Americans were a merciful people; otherwise, he said, they would have hanged him in 1765 when he supported the stamp tax. Drayton refused to duel with his belligerent opponent on the ground that as a congressman he was not accountable for his public declarations.[50]

Later Lee had some friendly correspondence with General Wayne, who, if he had not changed some of his opinions about the Battle of Monmouth, harbored no animosity. As tempers somewhat cooled, friends told Lee to be patient and assured him that sentiment would turn in his favor. But he was too impetuous for this kind of advice. "I must confess," he wrote, "I have not philosophy sufficient to conquer the resentment boiling in my breast." But notwithstanding how badly the country had used him he vowed that he would "always be a champion for the great righteous cause of American liberty."[51]

In December, 1779, after again receiving a letter from Lee which was considered disrespectful, Congress voted to sever him from any further connection with the army of the United States. Congress was widely divided: five states voted for dismissal, four opposed it, and three were equally divided. Regretting his indiscretion, Lee wrote a letter of apology; it elicited no reply.[52]

Lee died just four years after his court-martial. Never during those four long, bitter years was his mind off the tragic sequence of events which began at Monmouth, even though he penned essays on philosophical subjects and on the character of political institutions. He had an abiding fear, brought on by his martyrdom, that America was headed for arbitrary government. "For God's sake." he warned Richard Henry Lee in April 1782, "do not talk of Liberty until you have established the fundamental points, the limitation of power of the Assembly and the full freedom of the Press.[53]

In his will, witty and cynical to the last, he asked not to be buried in any churchyard or within a mile of a Presbyterian or Anabaptist meetinghouse. "For since I have resided in this country," he wrote, "I have kept so much bad company when living, that I do not choose to continue it when dead."[54]

At the end of his will, Lee, a man of the Enlightenment, summarized his thoughts on religion and God:

I recommend my soul to the Creator of all worlds and of all creatures; who must from his visible attributes, be indifferent to their modes of worship, or creeds, whether Christian, Mahometans, or Jews, whether instilled by education, or taken up by reflection; whether more or less absurd; a weak mortal can no more be answerable for his persuasions, notions, or even scepticism in religion, than for the colour of his skin.[55]

In his will Lee remembered Major John Francis Mercer and Colonel William Grayson with small gifts; they were, after all, men of wealth. Most of his livestock went to his faithful servant, Giuseppe Minghini. He also left some money for his housekeeper. His Virginia plantation, amounting to twenty-eight hundred acres, was divided among four of his friends: Major Edwards, who was then serving with Greene in the South, received a third; another third went to Jacob Morris, another former aide-de-camp; the remaining third was divided between Colonel Oswald and William Goddard, the Maryland printer who had stood by him throughout his tribulations. Property outside America went to his beloved sister, Sidney Lee, in England.[56]

A brief word about his death: he had come to Philadelphia to sell his plantation because it had become a burden to him. There he died of pneumonia on October 2, 1782. Shortly before his death, while staying at the Conestoga Inn, he happened to meet an old and destitute comrade of the Portugal campaign. Touched by the plight of his friend, but having no money, he sent his sword to be pawned; Robert Morris sent it back with the money, whereupon Lee wryly remarked, "Now, I hope you'll admit that my sword has done some good in America."[57]

In spite of the request in his will, his body was interred in the burying ground of Christ Church. At the funeral a very large crowd attended, including French dignitaries, among whom were the Duke de Lauzun and Barbé Marbois. For his part, Washington kindly wrote a letter of condolence to Sidney Lee.[58]

VI

In the Eyes of Historians

It may come as some surprise that the historians of the revolutionary generation were unusually unbiased in their appraisal of the events of the times in which they lived. Unlike many later historians, they did not regard George III as a tyrant or believe that the British people resolutely opposed any form of freedom in America. After a thorough examination of the available sources, they sifted the evidence and generally arrived at interpretations which have endured the test of time amazingly well.

The first writer to complete a history of the American Revolution was the Reverend William Gordon, a pastor, when the war began, of the Third Congregational Church of Roxbury, Massachusetts. A radical Whig, he was one of the first to advocate independence, while he was serving as chaplain of the Massachusetts Provincial Congress.

By 1776, convinced that the revolutionary movement would have worldwide significance as one of the great events in history, Gordon decided to gather all the information he could in anticipation of writing a history. Throughout the war, as he gathered material, he became a familiar figure in the camps and on the battlefields as well as in the halls of Congress. As the great drama unfolded, he acquired direct information from Washington and other knowledgeable persons. Then, after peace was made, he had free access to the papers of many of the principal participants.

Having written *The History of the Rise, Progress, and Establish-*

ment of the Independence of the United States of America, Gordon
went to London in 1786 to see to the publication of his manuscript; he
had concluded that there was too much prejudice in America to permit
an impartial history. To his surprise he found in England nearly as
much opposition to a fair appraisal of events. He was therefore com-
pelled to allow his manuscript to be edited several times before it was
finally published. Considering the times, nonetheless, his history re-
mains a remarkably impartial account of the Revolution.

Since 1899, the works of Gordon and other eighteenth- and early
nineteenth-century historians of the Revolution have been criticized, and
their histories have been charged with relying too heavily at times on the
Annual Register, an English publication dating from 1758. Since the
Annual Register generally made use of the best information available
(Edmund Burke wrote and compiled the section on history), Gordon and
other historians referred to it for matters concerning foreign affairs and
for aspects of the Revolution of which they had limited knowledge. As
for domestic events and the war in America, Gordon had his own partic-
ipation and observations as well as official documents and letters to
draw upon.

A perusal of the literature relating to the American Revolution re-
veals that Gordon's history influenced nearly all writers down to recent
times. The part dealing with Lee at Monmouth, on the other hand, has
been generally held to be obsolete since 1860, when there appeared
George Moore's revelations of Lee's indiscretion in giving General Howe
a plan for conquering America.

The account of Lee's conduct at Monmouth in Gordon's history
did not come from the *Annual Register,* which is noncommital as to
Lee's guilt or innocence.* It came rather from some unknown source
which appears no longer traceable. By way of introduction, Gordon
wrote: "Many were displeased with the conduct of the court martial:
and thought he ought not to have been found guilty except on the last
charge" [derogatory remarks about the commander in chief].

Then follows a long quotation explaining the reasons for Lee's retreat. It reads:

---

*The *Annual Register* states: "It is impossible for us to enter into the merits
of this sentence, in which party might have had a great share. When a dispute
had been carried to so great a height, between an officer on whom the Americans reposed their chief consequence, and one subordinate and less popular,
it is not difficult to divine where the blame will be laid." *Annual Register,*
1778, 226.

It appears from Washington's own letter and other circumstances, that it was submitted to Lee's judgment whether to attack, in what manner and when. There was manifest proof of Lee's intending to attack in hope of cutting off the enemy's covering party: but he altered his opinion as to the promising prospect he had of doing it, on his coming into the plain, reconnoitering the enemy, and concluding that they were more numerous than before supposed: and upon finding Scott had quitted the point of wood where he meant to order him to remain, he judged an immediate retreat necessary.

Continuing with an explanation of Lee's retreat, the passage reads:

The detachment with which Lee was, amounted to no more than one third of his whole command, Scott's column, Maxwell's brigade and the other troops to his left being full two-thirds. When he began to retire, the main body was more than six miles distant, though advancing. The enemy's force was rendered the more formidable by their great superiority in cavalry which was thought to be between four and five hundred. The ground being open was by no means advantageous to the Americans, as the British cavalry could have turned their flank. Would then an immediate attack under these circumstances, though it might have distressed the enemy's rear at the first onset, have been advisable, as it might probably have involved a general action before the detachment could have received support? Did not prudence dictate falling back and taking a new position, rather than hazarding an action in the plain? If Lee's judgment determined for the affirmative, how could he be declared guilty of disobeying orders? The circumstances already noted are in favor of the retreat's being necessary in the first instance: and when commenced, the prosecution of it was absolutely necessary till a good position could be taken for making an effectual stand against the enemy, to which position Lee was marching when met by Washington. The strenuous efforts of the British after the main army was drawn up in that position, before they retired three miles from the scene of action, tend also to justify the commencement of the retreat.

As to disorder during the retreat, the quotation had this to say:

No mention should have been made of its being in a few instances disorderly, unless such instances were really chargeable to Lee's misconduct; whereas of these few it is certain, that some were owing to fatigue and the enormous heat of the weather. The very sentence of the court martial is in favor of Lee's innocence as to the two first charges, for a year's suspension from command is no wise proportion to the crime if guilty.

After this quoted testimony absolving Lee from conducting a disorderly retreat, Gordon wrote:

Several are of opinion he would not have been condemned on these two, had it not been for his disrespectful conduct toward Washington. On the other hand, some have surmised, that his manoeuvers were owing either to treachery or want of courage: but they who have the opportunity of knowing him most, will be furthest from such apprehensions.[1]

Dr. David Ramsay's *History of the American Revolution,* published in 1789, was the next to appear. Four years before, he had published a history of the Revolution in South Carolina in which he gave Lee much credit for the defeat of the British at Charleston in 1776. More than Gordon, Ramsay is accredited with exceptional insights as a historian. His most recent evaluator, Page Smith, finds that Ramsay's interpretation of the causes of the American Revolution appears sounder than that of many twentieth-century historians.

Born in Lancaster County, Pennsylvania, Ramsay graduated from Princeton with talents, thought Benjamin Rush, "far superior to any person graduated at our college." After receiving a degree in medicine at the College of Philadelphia, he practiced medicine in Maryland before finally settling in Charleston, South Carolina. During the war, he served first as a representative in the South Carolina legislature and then as a delegate to Congress from his adopted state. Meanwhile he turned his encyclopedic mind to the collection of data and the writing of histories. Like Gordon, he was not averse to copying without noting his source, which was often the *Annual Register.* However, as a thoughtful evaluator of persons and events, Ramsay will always stand high among writers on American history.

A glance at Ramsay's treatment of Lee shows either that he followed closely the quotation in Gordon's work or that both used the same source. Some of the wording used by Ramsay is identical to Gordon's. Ramsay's version reads as follows:

Many were displeased with this sentence. They argued that by the tenor of Lee's orders, it was submitted to his discretion, whether to attack or not, and also, that the time and manner were to be determined by his own judgment. That at one time he intended to attack, but altered his opinion on apparently good grounds. That the propriety of an attack considering the superiority of the British cavalry, and the openness of the ground, was very questionable. That though it might have distressed the enemy's rear in the first instance; it would probably have brought on a general action, before the advanced corps could have been supported by the main body, which was some miles in the rear. If, said they, Lee's judgment was against attacking the enemy, he could not be guilty of disobeying an order for that purpose, which was suspended on the condition of his own approbation of the measure. They also agreed that a suspension from command, was not sufficient punishment for his crimes, if really guilty. They therefore inferred a presumption of his innocence from the lenient sentence of his judges. Though there was a diversity of opinions relative to the first and second charges, all were agreed in pronouncing him guilty of disrespect to the commander-in-chief. The Americans had formerly idolized Gen. Lee, but some of them now went to the opposite extreme, and pronounced him treacherous and deficient in courage, though there was no foundation for either of these suspicions. His temper was violent and his impatience of subordination had led him often to quarrel with those whom he was bound to respect and obey: but his courage and fidelity could not be questioned.[2]

The next publication was Edward Langworthy's brief sketch entitled *A Memoir of Major General Lee,* printed in London in 1792. A Georgian by birth, Langworthy had been a schoolteacher before the Revolution. At the beginning of the Revolutionary movement, he took the Tory side but soon changed his mind and became a prominent leader of the radical Whigs of Georgia. In 1777, he became a Georgia delegate to the Continental Congress, where he audaciously defended Lee when his sentence was reviewed by Congress. In 1785, Langworthy joined William Goddard in publishing the *Maryland Journal and Baltimore Advertiser.* Goddard, one of Lee's loyal friends, had acquired the latter's papers after his death; from these Langworthy constructed his life of Lee.

A reading of Lee's papers strengthened Langworthy's opinion that the general had been deeply wronged by his judges. Lee, wrote Langworthy,

gave up security for insecurity, certainty for uncertainty; . . . he staked all on the die of her [America's] fortune; if she succeeded, he could not be better; if she miscarried, his whole was lost.

The most difficult task [in preparing the biography] was not giving offence to such characters as had been the objects of Lee's aversion and resentment. . . . Lee's disappointment, unhappily, had soured his temper; the affair at Monmouth . . . and other things had gotten the better of his philsophy . . . and he became, as it were, angry with all mankind. . . . Humanity will draw a veil over his involuntary errors of sensibility, and pardon the sallies of a suffering mind.[3]

Langworthy's sympathetic treatment of Lee was followed by *The History of the Origin, Progress, and Termination of the American War* by Charles Stedman, a British officer who had served in various campaigns in the course of the war. Like Gordon and Ramsay, Stedman at times leaned heavily on the *Annual Register* but, with the others, his history contains the insights of a man who had seen much of the war at first hand.

Stedman had high praise for Lee's generalship at Monmouth.

The conduct of General Lee on this day, which was so severely arraigned, and unjustly punished by the Americans, was worthy of applause and admiration. He had been betrayed across some narrow passes of a marsh by the persuasion that he had to deal with a rear-guard of only two or three battalions, when he suddenly perceived six thousand men, including the British light-infantry and grenadiers, forming to receive him. He retired with such quickness of decision, though not attacked, that he repassed the marsh before our line was in readiness to move. Had he, in expectation of support, maintained his ground on the plain, until the British had attacked him, he must have been overpowered, and would not have had any retreat.

Stedman undertook to show how Washington failed to capitalize on his advantages by Lee's retreat:

The check [Lee's retreat] that the advanced guard of the American army sustained did not appear to be so great as to justify a declination of all farther attempts against the British army, even at that very time. Having come up with the main body of his army, fresh and untired troops, he [Washington] should have endeavoured to turn one of General Clinton's flanks. Had he succeeded, that part of the British army must have been destroyed. . . . Yet in such a conjecture of affairs, it was observed the British general risked, and even courted an action, while the American General suffered the important occasion to pass by, when he might have terminated the war by one great and decisive effort.[4]

The first writer to condemn Lee for his conduct at Monmouth was the Reverend Mason Locke Weems, the originator of the story of Washington and the cherry tree. Weems's account of what happened at Monmouth comprised all the wild stories that had circulated since the day of the battle.

Born in Maryland, Weems was one of the first two Americans to be ordained in England for service in the Episcopal church in the United States. For a while he held a pulpit in Maryland, but he soon became so interested in editing, writing, and selling books that he eventually devoted all his time to these activities. His life of Washington, a fictionalized biography, became a best seller and with some variations went through seventy editions.

Here is the way Weems pictured the dramatic encounter between Washington and Lee at Monmouth.

But, as he advanced, to his infinite astonishment he met Lee retreating, and the enemy pursuing. "For God's sake, General Lee," said Washington with great warmth, "what is the cause of this ill-timed prudence?" "No man, sir," replied Lee, quite convulsed with rage, "can boast a larger portion of that rascally virtue than your Excellence!" Dashing along by the madman, Washington rode up to his troops, who, at the sight of him rent the air with "God save great Washington!" "My brave fellows," said he, "can you fight?" They answered with three cheers! "Then face about, my heroes, and charge."[5]

One may interpose here that, if one is to judge some modern writers' interpretation of the events at Monmouth, their only source of reference must be Parson Weems.

Following the appearance of Weems's life of Washington, Chief Justice John Marshall, who had fought at the Battle of Monmouth as an officer in the Virginia line, brought out his three volumes on the life of Washington. He took pains to explain in a most favorable light Lee's reasons in the councils of war for opposing a general battle:

General Lee was decisively of opinion that, with such an equality of forces, it would "be criminal" to hazard an action. He relied much on the advantageous ground in which their late foreign connections had placed the United States, and strongly underscored that only a defeat of their army could now endanger their independence. To this he said the army ought not be exposed. It would be impossible, he thought, to bring on a partial action, without risking its being made general, if such should be the choice of the enemy, since the detachment which would engage must be supported, or be cut to pieces. A general action ought not to be fought, unless the advantage was manifestly with the American army. This at present was by no means the case.

In his strong support of the general, he added that Lee

soon perceived himself, to have been mistaken in the force which formed the rear of the British, yet he proposed to engage on that ground, although his judgment, as was afterwards stated by himself in an inquiry into his conduct, disapproved of it, there being a morass immediately in his rear, which could not be passed without difficulty, and which would necessarily impede the arrival of reenforcements to his aid, and embarrass his retreat should he be finally overpowered.

Marshall thought, like Gordon and Ramsay, that Lee by reason of his disrespectful letters to Washington had brought about his own downfall. A public examination probably never would have taken place, he wrote, had Lee's "proud spirit have stooped to offer explanation instead of outrage, to the Commander-in-Chief." The army, said Marshall, welcomed his suspension from the service because of his insults to Washington. Indeed, it would have been difficult for him to have remained in the army, Marshall thought, were he acquitted by the court.[6]

About the time John Marshall's life of Washington appeared, Abiel Holmes, a noted Congregational minister and the father of Oliver Wendell Holmes, the essayist, brought out in two volumes his *American Annals,* perhaps the first attempt "at an extensive orderly history of the country as a whole." His description of the Battle of Monmouth has the care and attention to details which characterize the entire history. After reaching Freehold, "Lee now perceived," wrote Holmes, "that he had mistaken the force, which formed the rear of the British, but he still proposed to engage on that ground. While both armies were preparing for action, General Scott, mistaking an oblique march of an American column for a retreat, left his position, and repassed a morass in his rear." The conclusion is that Lee was a man of "solid judgement" and "undaunted bravery." Holmes did not comment on the court-martial, an omission which may mean that he did not approve of the decision and preferred not to discuss it.[7]

The next work to appear was Henry (Light-Horse Harry) Lee's *Memoirs of the War in the Southern Department of the United States.* Lee (who was not related to the general) served throughout the war but was not present during the engagement at Monmouth. Like his son, Robert E. Lee, Henry had military talents of a high order, a fact which makes his support of Lee's generalship at Monmouth particularly interesting.

Henry Lee wrote:

[General Lee,] concluding that he should most effectively answer the object of Washington by drawing the enemy to him, thus inducing the foe to expend his bodily strength, while he saved that of the American army, in a day of uncommon heat, instantly began to retrograde; to take which step he had additionally induced by discerning that the corps on his flank, under Brigadier Scott, had repassed the ravine in his rear. [He] continued to retire, making good his retreat without injury, and exposing his person to every danger.

After clearing General Lee of the charges against his generalship, Henry Lee, like the others, deprecated his intemperate language in the tilt with Washington.[8]

A few years after the appearance of Lee's history, another penetrating work was written by Paul Allen and two associates, John Neal and Tobias Watkins. Although Allen was a writer of some note (who contributed to the Philadelphia *Port Folio*), he seems to have left a great deal of the writing of the history to his colleagues.

Whoever was responsible for it wrote a passage in Allen's history that constitutes one of the strongest vindications of Lee to be found:

There can be no doubt that the orders given to Lee, reserved to him a discretionary power. If indeed he had obeyed them, without attending to the "very powerful reasons" which forbade it, he must have lost his whole division. . . .

Regarding the charge that Lee conducted a cowardly and disorderly retreat, the book has this to say:

The second charge was totally contrary to the fact, so wholly repugnant to the life and character of General Lee, so inconsistent with the conduct of the many brave and excellent officers in his division, that the decision of the Court becomes perfectly enigmatical . . . Surely, they could not have thought to gratify the Commander-in-Chief by disgracing General Lee? And yet we shall search in vain into the recesses of the human heart, for any other motive, which could have induced them to defy truth, justice and fact.[9]

Allen's history was followed by another judicious account in William Johnson's life of Nathanael Greene. After discussing the court-martial and the sentence, Johnson, a South Carolina judge, had this to say:

This issue is well known, Lee was suspended from command; but whilst impartial posterity shall condemn the insubordination of his letters to the commander-in-chief, they will probably decide strongly in favor of the propriety of his conduct in retreating when he did. . . . Perhaps it was the real cause of the partial success which ensued.[10]

Other histories and biographies of note written in this period agreed with the view that Lee was guilty only of disrespect. Among these were the histories by John H. Hinton, Thomas Gordon, Robert Waln, Joel Tyler Headly, and Washington Irving.[11] A number of diaries and memoirs also appeared which accepted this interpretation. The most notable of these were by Dr. James Thacher and Alexander Graydon. The latter, who knew Lee, said that he did not consider his conduct at Monmouth "unmilitary." "I would rather suppose," he wrote, "if he committed a fault, it was because he was to respectful of the enemy, and that he was too scientific, too much of a reasoner for a merely executive officer."[12]

Of the scholarly writers whose works appeared before 1860, Jared Sparks is the last to be considered. As a professor at Harvard, Sparks was at the height of his career as a historian, biographer, and editor when he published a life of Washington in which he went counter to prevailing thought by criticizing Lee for his retreat at Monmouth. Lee, wrote Sparks, ran "the hazard of throwing all parts of the army into confusion at the moment when the enemy was pressing upon him with unimpeded force."[13]

Some years later Sparks wrote a short biography of Lee. After studying Lee's papers, he now changed his mind and agreed that Lee's generalship warranted praise at Monmouth. After flatly stating that Lee's orders were discretionary, he wrote:

The truth seems to have been that the extreme heat of the weather, the consequent fatigue of the men, and the nature of the ground, caused some of the troops to move in scattered manner; whilst others, under more favorable circumstances, marched regularly and in compact formation."

Sparks explained why he thought the court brushed aside the evidence and convicted Lee on all three counts. First of all, "the disrespectful and even insulting language which he had allowed himself to use in his two letters to Washington could not be overlooked nor easily forgiven." This, and the memory that Lee had not responded to Washington's call as soon as desired during the retreat across New Jersey in 1776 "helped to foster the apprehension of a sinister design, on his part, to effect the ruin of Washington, with the ambitious hope of becoming his successor."[14]

An abrupt and startling change in the interpretation of Lee's career occurred in 1860, when George Moore revealed the plan for conquering America which Lee submitted to General Howe while the former was a captive in New York. Moore, then the director of the Lenox Library, was convinced that here was incontestable proof that Lee, disgruntled at not being made commander in chief of the Continental army at the beginning of the war, had all along plotted against Washington and had been at heart a traitor ever since he failed to answer promptly Washington's call for help during the retreat through New Jersey.

Entitled *The Treason of Charles Lee,* Moore's book begins with the emphatic declaration in the preface that "This Essay . . . presents to the world, for the first time, the positive proofs of the treason of General Lee. . . ."[15]

After this devastating attack, few cared to defend Lee or find anything worthwhile in his entire life. With Moore's findings at hand, George Washington Parke Custis, a nineteenth-century playwright of some note, at once joined in the attack on Lee. Custis, who was born in 1781, lived with Washington at Mount Vernon since his father, who was Martha Washington's son, had died. He met many veterans of the Revolution and in 1824 entertained Lafayette on his visit to America. To support his condemnation of Lee, Custis cited Elias Boudinot, who—like Laurens, Hamilton, and Lafayette—was suspicious of Lee after the Battle of Monmouth. One suspects also that Custis was influenced by Parson Weems; he wrote dramatically that Colonel Hamilton leaped from his horse at Monmouth and, drawing his sword, addressed Washington as follows: "We are betrayed, your Excellency and the army are betrayed, and the moment has arrived when every friend of America and her cause must be readied to die in their defense."[16]

Benson J. Lossing, who combined skill in art with that of writing, followed the new trend in negative evaluation. A dozen years earlier, when his *Pictorial Field Book of the Revolution* first appeared, he suspected that Lee's motives were not of the best.

The conduct of Lee throughout the day was very strange and gives a coloring of truth to the conjecture that the thorn of envy was still rankling in his bosom, and that he preferred seeing the Americans disgraced by a defeat, rather than Washington honored by a victory.[17]

This, no doubt, came from reading Weems or from heeding some of the old gossip spread by Lee's enemies.

After the appearance of Moore's *Treason of Charles Lee,* Lossing condemned Lee without reservation. "The proof of this [Lee's treason]," he wrote, "has been recently discovered." Lee now deserved, he declared, to be "ranked with Church and Arnold, among the traitors whose deeds stain the annals of the American Revolution."[18]

When the distinguished historian George Bancroft had published in 1866 his volume on the War of Independence, he accepted without reservation the opinions and interpretations of Moore, Lossing, and Custis: "While the American army was pining from the delinquency of the states to meet the requisitions of Congress, Lee, then second in command was treacherously plotting its ruin." Bancroft completely ignored Lee's praiseworthy defense of the line in front of the west morass. After Washington had placed Stewart and Ramsay in position, "he again met Lee, who was doing nothing . . . and finding in him no disposition to retrieve his character, ordered him to the rear."[19]

John Fiske, another historian of nineteenth-century fame, was equally critical. Fiske called Lee's retreat at Monmouth "shameful"; like Bancroft, he was not always careful of his facts. For example, Fiske asserts that the retreat was "ordered" by Lee, who was left "cowering and trembling in his stirrups" after his encounter with Washington. In conclusion he states unequivocally that Washington was robbed of a great victory by the treachery of Charles Lee.[20]

Another prominent historian and biographer, Charlemagne Tower, wrote in his life of Lafayette that Lee's "treacherous proceedings . . . came very near being the means . . . of bringing unmeasurable disaster upon the Continental army at Monmouth." Lee, he maintained, was always an Englishman at heart and could be depended upon to aid the enemy whenever an opportunity appeared.[21]

Toward the end of the century, Woodrow Wilson joined the ranks of Lee's detractors. The future president of the United States wrote that Clinton

might never have reached New York at all had not Charles Lee been once more second in command of the American army. He had come out of captivity, exchanged, and now proved himself the insubordinate poltroon he was. He had never had any real heart in the cause. . . . While a prisoner he had secretly directed Howe's movement against Philadelphia, and now he was to consummate his cowardly treachery.[22]

Another voice in the rising chorus against Lee was that of Moses Coit Tyler, author of the classic *Literary History of the American Revolution*. With the verve for which he was known, Tyler wrote of "that brilliant and Mephistophelean personage" whose "treason" was "perhaps more profligate, and certainly more damaging, than that of Benedict Arnold. . . ."[23]

Notwithstanding the great outcry against Lee, there were still some writers who questioned the conclusions of Moore and his followers and more or less favored the interpretation current before 1860. One of these was Henry B. Carrington, a brigadier general during the Civil War. In his *Battles of the American Revolution,* he concluded that

a careful examination of the facts seems to exclude the idea that Lee was guilty of any overt act of treason, while it is equally true, that upon the basis of his antecedent opinion, and his expectation of failure, he did not make the proper effort to render the failure the least disastrous possible, and thus, fulfill the obligation of high command.[24]

William Stryker, another historian with a military background, spent many years studying the battles of Trenton, Princeton, and Monmouth. Like Carrington, Stryker found no good reason to believe that Lee had committed treason at Monmouth. Lee's orders, he noted, were discretionary and there was nothing in his conduct during the advance or retreat that could be called unmilitary. "General Lee," he summed up, "deserves credit for self-possession and a real purpose to bring the men away in safety. . . ."[25]

Stryker, it should be pointed out, was not the first after the appearance of Moore's book to defend Lee's military actions in so sweeping a manner. Indeed, as early as 1861, only a year after Moore's work was published, Winthrop Sargent, a Philadelphian long noted for his history of the Braddock campaign and for a life of Major John André, wrote that "in common justice . . . to the reputation of the turbulent and irregular Lee, whose prestige was on this day so fatally damaged, I must acknowledge that his conduct before the enemy seems to me to have been unworthy of the censure it received."[26]

Shortly after the turn of the century, Lee was again strongly defended by another Philadelphian, Sydney George Fisher. In his opinion, the judgment of Fiske and others that Lee courted defeat at Monmouth so that Washington would be ruined was nothing less than fanciful thinking. It is true, he admitted,

that Lee's character was, in many respects, a contemptible one, and that his conduct when a prisoner was of a very treacherous complexion; . . . from that one cannot infer that he contemplated treachery at Monmouth unless there are some positive facts tending to show it.

Fisher concluded that

an impartial view of all the evidence of the witnesses at the court-martial afterwards held, together with the accounts of the battle given by the British, fail to show that Lee was in fault. His retreat seems to have been both fortunate and necessary. At the moment when Washington met him, he had brought the troops out of a bad strip of country about two and a half miles in length, in which all the positions were favorable to the British, and he had just reached a good position to make a stand.

Washington, Fisher felt, would not have brought charges against Lee had not the latter, stung by cruel injustice, written his "injudicious" letters.[27]

Regardless of Fisher's defense of Lee, his contemporaries continued to read the worst of motives in Lee's behavior. Francis Vinton Greene, a West Pointer and army officer who became a historian and biographer, took pains to describe how Washington and his officers worked hard to get the army ready for battle during the long winter at Valley Forge. But at Monmouth, he wrote, all was in danger of being lost "by the combined incapacity, cowardice and treason of this damnable Charles Lee."

Arnold's treason, Greene concluded, was "but a slight fraction of the mischief caused by Lee on this hot Sunday morning at Monmouth." Disregarding the fact that Washington was not within supporting distance, he came to the astonishing conclusion that

In spite of Clinton's superiority, had Lee attacked him vigorously and held him at the Court House until Washington came up, Washington would have passed around Clinton's right flank between Monmouth and Middletown, and in all probability have captured a large part of Clinton's command.[28]

Wayne Whipple, a biographer of Washington, was as emphatic as Greene in his condemnation.

Lee's orders from Washington were positive and explicit. He was to gain the flank of the British left wing and attack it vigorously, while Washington was to come up and complete its discomfiture. Lee's force was ample, in quantity and quality, for the task assigned to it, and there was fair ground for hope that the flower of the British army might thus be cut off and captured and destroyed. Since the war began there had hardly been such a golden opportunity.

Whipple ended with a savage denunciation of Lee. The light sentence which Lee received, he thought, was the result of that "ill-judged humanity which has been wont to characterize judicial proceedings in America." In Europe Lee would have been shot. Lee, in fact, "was nothing but a selfish adventurer. He had no faith in the prinicples for which the Americans were fighting, or indeed any principles."[29]

Joining the detractors of Lee, the noted Harvard historian Edward Channing wrote in 1912: "Then Lee made some incomprehensible and wholly disastrous movements which lost to the American soldiers the advantage they had gained and gave the enemy a chance to threaten their left flank."[30] One of Channing's contemporaries, Claude Van Tyne, an authority on the American Revolution, was certain that victory within Washington's grasp at Monmouth was "lost by the treachery or cowardice of General Lee."[31]

Since 1940 many prominent historians have written about the American Revolution and, like most of their predecessors since 1860, have been highly critical of Lee. Carl Van Doren, the eminent biographer, wrote that the Americans under Lee were in great confusion when Washington appeared. "This again," said Van Doren, "might look more like treason in Lee if his retreat had not been in keeping with his fixed theory that American troops were no match for the British except in guerrilla skirmishes." Furthermore Lee's fraternizing with the British when a captive among them "had made him indecisive, and his indecision at Monmouth was, in effect, treachery."[32]

Christopher Ward, author of a comprehensive and generally authoritative history of the War for Independence, gave Lee no credit at all. During the retreat, Ward maintained that Lee was enjoying the quiet satisfaction of "I told you so," when Washington appeared on the scene.[33] Like Ward, John C. Miller, author of several books on the Revolution, termed Lee a bungler rather than a traitor. His chief mistake, Miller wrote, was in ordering a retreat before the action had fairly begun. In effect, he was beaten before the battle began by giving the British too much credit for their fighting ability.[34] Another historian writing in the 1940's was Nathaniel W. Stephenson, whose estimation of Lee was also derogatory. "But even Lee," he wrote, "whether fool or traitor, dared not give up so easily." His gallant defense of the line in front of the west morass, he hinted, was but a pretense to cover up his duplicity.[35]

In the 1950's, Bruce Lancaster, a writer of popular books, pictured Lee as totally incompetent:

Charles Lee, master of the art of war, scattered his units over the broken terrain like confetti spilling from a sack. There was no plan of attack, no direction, and most of the details of this part of the day may be reconstructed only by surmise and conjecture.[36]

Another writer on the popular side, Fairfax Downey, fully agrees with Lancaster. As he describes the action,

Lafayette's and Wayne's brigade struck Clinton's rear guard near Freehold, Monmouth County, New Jersey. Steadily volleys and cannon fire were breaking the redcoat's ranks when General Charles Lee, a former British officer, treacherously ordered a retreat. The Americans fell back in raging confusion.[37]

North Callahan, who wrote on Generals Knox and Morgan, thought that Lee's troops retreated in wild confusion. He also assumed that Lee ordered the retreat when all was going well for the Americans. But he did admit that some contemporary historians viewed Lee's actions "in a more favorable light than was the tendency for many years."[38]

Douglas Southall Freeman, the competent biographer of Robert E. Lee, apparently detested Charles Lee. Regarding his generalship, Freeman saw nothing but ineptitude, although he did not accuse him of treason and cowardice.[39] Another biographer, Broadus Mitchell, agreed with Freeman that Lee's retreat was entirely unwarranted. He also agreed that Lee disobeyed orders but, like Freeman, he did not go so far as to accuse him of treason or cowardice.[40]

During the 1960's more historians and biographers condemned Lee in one degree or another. Like Freeman and Mitchell, two army officers, Colonel R.E. and Colonel T.N. Dupuy, saw Monmouth as a clear victory for Washington had not Lee disobeyed the commander in chief and ordered a disastrous retreat.[41]

The distinguished historian Samuel Eliot Morison wrote in the *Oxford History of the American People* that Lee disobeyed and retreated "with so little reason as to be suspected of treason."[42] Like Morison, Alfred Hoyt Bill, in writing for the New Jersey Tercentennial, found Lee guilty beyond a doubt: "He was convicted on all three counts but the sentence was ridiculously inadequate."[43] Writing in a more popular vein, Lieutenant Colonel Joseph B. Mitchell found Lee rather content with the way things had gone:

Some units formed for attack, others began to retreat. General Lee seemed quite pleased by developments. Perhaps he believed that his point had been proved. Americans were not yet trained to face British bayonets.[44]

James T. Flexner, the most recent of Washington's biographers, believes that Lee was neither a traitor nor a coward. The trouble lay in a basic disagreement between Washington and Lee on the fighting power of the Continental and British soldiers.

Washington, resolute as always since he had finally made up his mind, agreed that only Lee's pusillanimousness had prevented a major American triumph. He scorned Lee's claim to have saved the army from disaster. Who was right? The way the Continental Army, when Washington had finally rallied them, stood up to the enemy implies that Lee's mental confusion and lack of confidence with American soldiery had served the enemy well.[45]

Having surveyed the writings of recent historians who portrayed Lee in an unfavorable light, let us turn to historians who believe the truth about Lee to be much nearer to the interpretation drawn by Gordon and Ramsay nearly two centuries ago. One who, it would seem, carefully studied the evidence, was W.E. Woodward. He writes:

Clinton's reports, published after the war, show that the whole British army was about to fall on Lee's four thousand men. It seems in the light of this fact that the retirement of his force was a most necessary thing to do. At Lee's back there was a morass which could be crossed only by a road on a high embankment.

As to Washington, Woodward wrote: "It seems clear that Washington did not understand the situation and was too much annoyed and too hot to find out what it was." He also gave Lee credit for his defense of the line at the west morass:

The weight of expert opinion was that Lee was guilty only of disrespect to Washington, but he made a political issue of the incident and discussed Washington's failings as a soldier in public while the trial was going on. In short, his conduct was defiant and silly. The court felt, evidently, that it had to convict him on all three charges. . . .

Woodward also analyzed Lee's conduct at New York while he was a prisoner in the hands of the British. "This good fellowship among old comrades led him one day to display his vanity by writing out a plan for the conquest of America." "I think," concluded Woodward, "Lee was not so much a traitor as an eccentric." He "may not have attached much importance to his treasonable action in suggesting a campaign to the British. He may have considered it a kind of amusement, or a sort of imperial puzzle which he was vain enough to believe he could solve."
His actions at Monmouth, Woodward thought

do not reveal a traitorous intention. He could have had his whole command . . . nearly half of Washington's army . . . captured or badly defeated by simply obeying Washington's orders and remaining where he was. But he saved his troops by retiring with them, and this retirement led to the quarrel that ended his career."[46]

John Hyde Preston, a novelist and a writer of popular history and biography, agreed with Woodward. Preston wrote:

But, in the light of facts, it seems certain that if Lee had not retreated and had explicitly obeyed the orders he had, his whole command would have been listed among the killed and captured.[47]

Foremost among the scholars who have delved deeply into Lee's life and career is John Richard Alden. In his life of Lee, Alden found that the latter, threatened by a flanking movement, brought his corps back safely and thereby maneuvered the British into a hopeless position. Alden apparently believed that Lee was correct when he said that he gave Washington the only victory he had ever tasted, excluding the surprise attacks on Trenton and Princeton. At Monmouth, Alden judged, Washington's strategy was faulty and censurable.

When Lee confronted Washington after the battle, in Alden's opinion, he did not realize that he had no chance against the commander in chief even though the facts supported him. As to the exchange of letters between Lee and Washington:

Although its purpose was not of a nature to please the commander-in-chief and in spite of the fact it contained much self praise, Lee's letter to Washington was couched in respectful terms and expressed the belief that Washington would not knowingly commit an injustice. The commander in chief's reply was contemptuous in tone and vindictive in content. His notice that Lee would be accused of having made a shameful retreat indicates animus against his subordinate and a disposition to hurt him as much as possible.[48]

In his most recent book on the Revolution, published in 1969, Alden sums up the dilemma confronting the court at Lee's trial. "On the face of it," he writes, "Lee could hardly be guilty, yet it would not do to exculpate him. His service had been substantial, but he had been insubordinate and creative of mischief."[49]

Another present-day historian who comes out strongly in defense of Lee's generalship at Monmouth is William B. Willcox. In his *Portrait of a General: Sir Henry Clinton in the War of Independence,* he writes that Clinton's troops, "among the best that the world of the day produced, outnumbered Lee's by roughly three to two; if he could throw the enemy back quickly into the defiles, before help could reach them, they would be in serious trouble. And Washington was hours away."

As to Lee's retreat,

General Lee, fighting doggedly and keeping his troops intact, fell back across the western ravine. By the time Clinton reached the final one, he was too late to win even a partial victory.

Willcox offers no comments on Lee's trial.[50]

John Shy, of the University of Michigan, has also closely studied the record. He writes:

But no one who carefully reads the record of the trial, examines the ground, and considers the British side of the battle would find Lee guilty of the first two charges. But no one who reads his letters to Washington will believe him innocent of the third. Under the circumstances an acquittal on the first two charges would have been a vote of no confidence in Washington.[51]

The most recent biography of Lee, written by Samuel White Patterson, was published in 1958. He, too, found that Lee was unjustly convicted and that his retreat at Monmouth was militarily sound. Speaking of Lee's place in history, Patterson wrote:

When that day of justice arrives, a stone or tablet should mark his all but forgotten resting place. Maybe there will be subscribed, that all may read, a translation of the Latin wording on the Dublin tomb of Lee's mentor and fellow egotist, Jonathan Swift: "No longer does bitterest indignation gnaw his heart; Stranger, passing by, go and emulate if you can his strenuous defense of the liberty of mankind."[52]

Of Washington, James Parton, a nineteenth-century biographer, wrote: "He was as fond of adulation as he was known to be sensitive of censure, and . . . no officer could stand well with him who did not play the part of worshipper."[53] Lee by temperament was one who could not be a worshipper of any man.

Though not unaware of the great veneration for Washington, Lee somehow imagined that by an appeal to a "candid world" he would be vindicated. But to have acquitted Lee of the charges made against him by Washington following the Battle of Monmouth would have constituted an affront to the commander in chief. This neither the court nor the Congress was prepared to do. Rather, in effect, they allowed him to become Washington's scapegoat.

Notes

CHAPTER ONE: WASHINGTON AND LEE

1. Gottschalk, *Lafayette Joins*, 16.
2. Graydon, *Memoirs*, 299-300.
3. Greene, *Nathanael Greene*, II, 30-31.
4. Chitwood, *Richard Henry Lee*, 215.
5. Knollenberg, *Washington and the Revolution*, 78-91; Adams, *Familiar Letters*, I, 264; Thayer, *Nathanael Greene*, 215ff.
6. Adams, *Works*, III, 93; Chitwood, *Richard Henry Lee*, 218.
7. James Lovell to Horatio Gates, Nov. 7, 1777, Gates Papers, Box 8, NYPL.
8. Benjamin Rush MSS, XXIX, 136, Philadelphia Public Library; Fitzpatrick, *Writings of Washington*, XI, 164.
9. Burnett, *Letters*, III, 201, 204.
10. Fitzpatrick, *Writings of Washington*, XI, 164-165.
11. George Lux to Nathanael Greene, May 26, 1778, Greene Collections, II, William Clements Library.
12. Letters of Richard Peters, Jan. 29, 1778, Wayne Papers, Historical Society of Pennsylvania.
13. Gordon, *History of the Rise, Progress, and Establishment of the Independence of the United States*, II, 308.
14. Thacher, *Military Journal*, 156.
15. Sargent, *Major John André*, 179-180; Gordon, *History of the Rise, Progress, and Establishment of the Independence of the United States*, II, 327-328; Montresor, *Journal*, 492-493.
16. Cook, *What Manner of Men*, 37; Reed, *Joseph Reed*, I, 418-420.
17. "Letters from Major Baurmeister," 176-177; Donehoo, *Pennsylvania*, III, 118; Reed, *Joseph Reed*, I, 418-419.
18. Alden, *Charles Lee*, 165-166.
19. *Ibid.*; *Lee Papers*, IV, 135-136.

20. *Ibid.,* II, 376; "Letters from Major Baurmeister," 38, 52; Belcher, *The First American Civil War,* II, 196.

21. *Lee Papers,* II, 358-360; Moore, *The Treason of Charles Lee,* 105.

22. Burnett, *Letters,* II, 299-300; Thayer, *Nathanael Greene,* 160-161.

23. *Lee Papers,* II, 358-360, 368; Alden, *Charles Lee,* 171-172.

24. Anderson, *The Command of the Howe Brothers,* 221-222; Alden, *Charles Lee,* 175; *Lee Papers,* II, 361-368.

25. *Lee Papers,* IV, 163; Frost, *The Battle Grounds of America,* 147-148; Hillard, *The Last Men of the Revolution,* 42.

26. Irving, *Life of Washington,* III, 446.

27. Alden, *Charles Lee,* 303-306.

28. *Lee Papers,* I, 74.

29. *Ibid.,* I, 8, IV, 353.

30. *Ibid.,* I, 5.

31. Moore, *The Treason of Charles Lee,* 8; Alden, *Charles Lee,* 8-9.

32. *Lee Papers,* I, 52-53.

33. *Ibid.,* I, 37ff; Moore, *The Treason of Charles Lee,* 19-20.

34. *Ibid.*

35. *Lee Papers,* IV, 165, I, 272-273.

36. *Ibid.,* I, 73.

37. *Ibid.,* I, 43.

38. *Ibid.,* IV, 322.

39. *Ibid.,* I, 134, 137.

40. Moore, *The Treason of Charles Lee,* 29.

41. *Ibid.,* 25.

42. Alden, *Charles Lee,* 73; Thayer, *Nathanael Greene,* 56.

43. Thayer, *Nathanael Greene,* 67, 73.

44. *Lee Papers,* IV, 165, I, 272-273.

45. Johnston, "The Campaign of 1776 around New York," 284.

46. *Lee Papers,* II, 306-306.

47. *Ibid.,* 288-289.

48. *Ibid.,* II, 293.

49. *Ibid.,* II, 295-296.

50. *Ibid.,* II, 296, 305-306; Fitzpatrick, VI, 305-306, 311-312.

51. *Lee Papers,* II, 319, 326, 329, 349.

52. *Ibid.,* II, 337, 341, 345.

53. *Ibid.,* II, 345-348.

54. *Ibid.,* II, 345

55. Boudinot, *Journal,* 78.

56. Burnett, *Letters,* III, II, 161; Alden, *Charles Lee,* 194-195; Thayer, *Nathanael Greene,* 240.

57. Alden, *Charles Lee,* 202.

58. Sargent, *Major John André,* 163-164; Serle, *Journal,* 305.

59. *Lee Papers,* II, 405-406.

60. *Lee Papers,* II, 388.

61. Kite, *Louis Lebèque Duportail*, 59–61.

62. *Lee Papers*, II, 403–404.

63. *Ibid.*, II, 399–405; Fitzpatrick, XII, 60–63.

64. Fitzpatrick, *Writings of Washington*, XII, 75.

CHAPTER II: THE MARCH TO MONMOUTH

1. Fitzpatrick, *Writings of Washington*, XII, 91.

2. *Minutes of the Governor's Privy Council of New Jersey*, I, 35.

3. Fitzpatrick, XII, 97.

4. Clinton, *American Rebellion*, 90ff.

5. *Ibid.*, 86; Eelking, *The German Allied Troops*, 135; Woodward, *George Washington*, 347.

6. Willcox, *Portrait of a General*, 226; Clinton, *American Rebellion*, 85.

7. Willcox, *Portrait of a General*, 224, 227–229; Clinton, *American Rebellion*, 88–89.

8. Serle, *Journal*, 299–301; Baurmeister, *Journals*, 179.

9. Stryker, *Battle of Monmouth*, 68–71; Simcoe, *Journal*, 72.

10. *Annual Register*, 1778, 220; André, *Journal*, 10; Stryker, *Battle of Monmouth*, 82-83.

11. Stryker, *Battle of Monmouth*, 89-90.

12. *Ibid.*, 84-85; Ellis, *Monmouth County*, 165; Lowell, *Hessians*, 213; Clinton, *American Rebellion*, pp. 90-91; *New Jersey Archives*, 2nd. Ser., II, *Newspaper Extracts* (1778), 279-280; *Proc. NJHS.*, 1st. ser., VII, 86.

13. Clinton, *American Rebellion*, 90-91; Stedman, *History*, 18-20; Lowell, *Hessian*, 213; Gordon, *History of the Rise, Progress, and Establishment of the Independence of the United States*, 355-356.

14. Fitzpatrick, XII, 113.

15. *Lee Papers*, IV, 302; Freeman, *George Washington*, V, 16; Alden, *Charles Lee*, 208-209.

16. Fitzpatrick, XII, 117.

17. Greene to Washington, June 24, 1778, Washington Papers, vol. 28, p. 35, Library of Congress.

18. Wayne to Washington, June 24, 1778, Wayne Papers, Historical Society of Pennsylvania: Stillé, *Anthony Wayne*, 143.

19. "Letters from Major Baurmeister," 41.

20. J. Sparks, *Correspondence*, IV, 553; Fitzpatrick, XII, 140; Stryker, *Battle of Monmouth*, 75-77; H.C. Lodge, *Works of Alexander Hamilton*, VIII, 68.

21. Orderly Book, No. 3, Huntington Library; Stryker, *Battle of Monmouth*, 98.

22. Fitzpatrick, XII, 121.

23. Syrett, *Hamilton Papers*, I, 503; Morris, *Hamilton*, 43.

24. Fitzpatrick, XII, 120-121n.

25. *Hamilton Papers*, I, 503-506.

26. Tower, *La Fayette*, II, 355.

27. Fitzpatrick, XII, 122-123.

28. Tower, *La Fayette*, I, 364.

29. H. Lee, *Memoirs of the War in the Southern Department*, I, 58.

30. *Lee Papers*, II, 417-418.

31. *Ibid.*, II, 422; Thomas Gordon, *Gazetteer of the State of New Jersey,* 171; Gottschalk, *Lafayette Joins,* 211; Tower, *La Fayette,* I, 361.

32. Stryker, *Battle of Monmouth,* 92-95; Ellis, *Monmouth County,* 168.

33. Callahan, *Daniel Morgan,* 162; Higgenbotham, *Daniel Morgan,* 88.

34. *Magazine of American History,* II, 408.

35. Stryker, *Battle of Monmouth,* 95; Clinton, *American Rebellion,* 90.

CHAPTER III: LEE'S ADVANCE AND RETREAT

1. Chitwood, *Richard Henry Lee,* 36-37; Stryker, *Battle of Monmouth,* 45.

2. Thayer, *Nathanael Greene,* 427.

3. *Lee Papers,* III, 3-4, 175.

4. Graydon, *Memoirs,* 325.

5. *Lee Papers,* III, 6-9, 143-144; Gordon, *History of the Rise, Progress, and Establishment of the Independence of the United States,* II, 256.

6. Carrington, *Battles of the American Revolution,* 425.

7. *Lee Papers,* III, 143, 163; Clinton, *American Rebellion,* 92.

8. Freeman, *George Washington,* V, 26; *Lee Papers,* III, 7-10, Marshall, *Life of Washington,* III, 17.

9. *Lee Papers,* III, 231; Freeman, *George Washington,* V, 26; Alden, *Charles Lee,* 213.

10. Fitzpatrick, *Writings of Washington,* XII, 127-128.

11. *Ibid.,* XII, 128.

12. Gordon, *History of the Rise, Progress, and Establishment of the Independence of the United States,* 256-258.

13. *Lee Papers,* III, 34, 131.

14. *Ibid.,* III, 140, 162-163.

15. Clinton, *American Rebellion,* 92; *Lee Papers,* III, 103, 144, 169, 179.

16. *Lee Papers,* III, 126, 144.

17. *Ibid.,* III, 51, 144.

18. *Ibid.,* II, 451; Eelking, *The German Allied Troops,* 158; Townsend, *John Laurens,* 74.

19. *Lee Papers,* III, 19, 120; Stillé, *Anthony Wayne,* 145.

20. André, *Journal,* 11.

21. Ingles, *Queen's Rangers,* 55-56.

22. Martin, *Narrative,* 91-95.

23. *Lee Papers,* III, 132-133.

24. Griffin, *Stephen Moylan,* 76.

25. Baurmeister, *Journals,* 192.

26. *Lee Papers,* III, 180-181.

27. *Ibid.,* III, 180; Thomas H. Montgomery, "The Battle of Monmouth, Described by D. James. McHenry," *Magazine of American History,* III, 357; Gottschalk, *Lafayette Joins,* 221.

28. *Lee Papers,* II, 162; Clinton, *American Rebellion,* 93.

29. Clinton, *American Rebellion,* 94.

30. *Lee Papers,* III, 19; Stryker, *Battle of Monmouth,* 152; Bass, *Green Dragoon,* 45; Clinton's Muster Roll at Navesink, July 3, 1778, Freehold Museum, Freehold, New Jersey.

31. Gordon, *History of the Rise, Progress, and Establishment of the Indepen-*

dence of the United States, 358–359. Ellis, *Monmouth County,* 172.

32. *Lee Papers,* III, 180–181; Stryker, *Battle of Monmouth,* 134.

33. Ellis, *Monmouth County,* 165.

34. Watson, *Annals of Philadelphia,* II, 284; Wickwire, *Cornwallis.*

35. *Lee Papers,* III, 180–181.

36. *Ibid.,* III, 15.

37. *Ibid.,* III, 28–29, 146, 157, 182; Alden, *Charles Lee,* 217; Fisher, *The Struggle for American Independence,* II, 183.

38. *Lee Papers,* III, 134–135.

39. Gottschalk, *Lafayette Joins,* 223.

40. Irving, *Life of Washington,* III, 433; Thomas Gordon, *Gazetteer of the State of New Jersey,* 272.

41. Willcox, *Portrait of a General,* 234; Clinton, *American Rebellion,* 94.

42. *Lee Papers,* III, 205; Clinton, *American Rebellion,* 96.

43. Steiner, *James McHenry,* 19.

44. Gordon, *History of the Rise, Progress, and Establishment of the Independence of the United States,* II, 359; Clinton, *American Rebellion,* 93.

45. Gottschalk, *Lafayette Joins,* 222–225.

46. *Lee Papers,* III, 29, 91.

47. *Ibid.,* III, 186–187; Williams, *Biography of Revolutionary Heroes,* 244.

48. *Lee Papers,* III, 186–187.

49. *Lee Papers,* III, 3.

50. *Ibid.,* III, 112.

51. Stryker, *Battle of Monmouth,* 175.

52. *Lee Papers,* III, 68, 71, 73.

53. Irving, *Life of Washington,* III, 427.

54. *Lee Papers,* III, 78, 81, 112.

55. Fisher, *The Struggle for American Independence,* II, 63; Martin, *Narrative,* 91–95.

56. Fisher, *The Struggle for American Independence,* II, 184.

57. Broadus Mitchell, *Alexander Hamilton,* 165–166.

58. *Lee Papers,* II, 433; III, 147; Custis, *Recollections,* 218n.

59. Syrett, *Hamilton Papers,* I, 476.

60. *Ibid.,* I, 512.

61. Marshall, *Life of Washington,* III, 22n.

62. Montgomery, "Battle of Monmouth," 357–360.

63. *Lee Papers,* III, 166–167, 173; Stryker, *Battle of Monmouth,* 187, 193; Freeman, *George Washington,* V, 29–30.

64. *Lee Papers,* III, 59, 61, 113; Stille, *Anthony Wayne,* 152.

65. *Lee Papers,* III, 113, 166, 188; Stryker, *Battle of Monmouth,* 187, 193. Shaw, *Journals,* 159.

66. *Lee Papers,* III, 61; Syrett, *Hamilton Papers,* I, 512; Miller, *Triumph of Freedom,* 324.

67. *Lee Papers,* III, 70, 113; Montgomery, "Battle of Monmouth," 363.

68. Stryker, *Battle of Monmouth,* 186; Montgomery, "Battle of Monmouth," 363.

69. *Lee Papers,* III, 84, 223.

NOTES

70. Syrett, *Hamilton Papers,* I, 476; *Lee Papers,* III, 114; Irving, III, 431.

CHAPTER IV: AN UNSPRUNG TRAP

1. Syrett, *Hamilton Papers,* I, 513; Stryker, *Battle of Monmouth,* 209.
2. *Lee Papers,* III, 81.
3. *Ibid.,* III, 147-148, 261.
4. *Lee Papers,* III, 96.
5. Custis, *Recollections,* 224.
6. Freeman, *George Washington,* V, 26.
7. Johnson, *Nathanael Greene,* I, 104.
8. *Lee Papers,* III, 71; Thomas Gordon, *Gazetteer of the State of New Jersey,* 273.
9. Stryker, *Battle of Monmouth,* 212-213; André, *Journal,* 13.
10. Stirling to William Henry Drayton, Aug. 15, 1778, *Proceedings of the New Jersey Historical Society,* LX (1942), 73; Stryker, *Battle of Monmouth,* 211-213; Callahan, *Henry Knox,* 145; Coffin, *The Lives and Services of Major General John Thomas,* et al., 119-120; Scheer and Rankin, *Rebels and Redcoats,* 331.
11. Stryker, *Battle of Monmouth,* 210.
12. Parton, *Aaron Burr,* 108; Aaron Burr, *Memoirs,* I, 127; Stryker, *Battle of Monmouth,* 210-211.
13. Elias Boudinot to his wife, June 30, 1778, NYPL: Custis, *Recollections,* 221-222; Clinton, *American Rebellion,* 94-95.
14. Stillé, *Anthony Wayne,* 147; Stryker, *Battle of Monmouth,* 216; Ellis, *Monmouth County,* 180; Custis, *Recollections,* 221; John Laurens, *Correspondence,* 195.
15. Ward, *Delaware Continentals,* 276; Stryker, *Battle of Monmouth,* 215-216; Salter and Beekman, *Old Times in Old Monmouth,* 159; Ellis, *Monmouth County,* 180; Montgomery, "Battle of Monmouth," 358.
16. Montgomery, "Battle of Monmouth," 358; Stryker, *Battle of Monmouth,* 220.
17. André, *Journal,* 73.
18. *Ibid.;* Stryker, *Battle of Monmouth,* 200-202.
19. Callahan, *Henry Knox, passim.*
20. John Watts De Peyster, "The Battle of Monmouth," *Magazine of American History,* II, 411-413.
21. Willcox, *Portrait of a General,* 236; *Proceedings of the New Jersey Historical Society,* First Series, VI, 18.
22. Montgomery, "Battle of Monmouth," 360.
23. Syrett, *Hamilton Papers,* I, 513.
24. Fitzpatrick, *Writings of Washington,* XII, 130-131.
25. *Lee Papers,* III, 260; Clinton, *American Rebellion,* 95-96.
26. Johnson, *Nathanael Greene.*
27. Fitzpatrick, *Writings of Washington,* XII, 126-127; *Lee Papers,* III, 120; Ellis, *Monmouth County,* 177n.
28. Graham, *Daniel Morgan,* 204; Ellis, *Monmouth County,* 176.
29. Moore, *Diary of the American Revolution,* II, 375, 524; Custis, *Recollections,* 308n.
30. Fisher, *The Struggle for American Independence,* II, 186; Callahan, *Henry*

Knox, 146; *New Jersey Archives, Newspapers Extracts* (1778), 268 (*Long Branch News*, Oct. 15, 1886); Williams, *Biography of Revolutionary Heroes*, 246.

31. Smith, *Battle of Monmouth*, 31-32; Montgomery, "Battle of Monmouth," 355; *George Clinton Papers*, III, 508; Dearborn, *Journal*, 178; Fisher, *The Struggle for American Independence*, II, 186; *Lee Papers*, II, 467; Stillé, *Anthony Wayne*, 153; Baurmeister, *Journal*, 186; Moore, *Diary of the American Revolution*, 69; Clinton, *American Rebellion*, 96n.

32. *New Jersey Archives, 2nd. ser., II, Newspaper Extracts* (1778), 268, 273-274; Clinton, *American Rebellion*, 96n; Stryker, *Battle of Monmouth*, 201; *George Clinton Papers*, III, 508.

33. Callahan, *Daniel Morgan*, 168, 319; Custis, *Recollections*, 226; Clinton, *American Rebellion*, 97; Stryker, *Battle of Monmouth*, 239; Ellis, *Monmouth County*, 181.

34. Annual Register, 1778, 227; *Stuart-Bute Correspondence*, 71; Fisher, *The Struggle for American Independence*, II, 187; Ellis, *Monmouth County*, 182; Gordon, *History of the Rise, Progress, and Establishment of the Independence of the United States*, II, 367. Quantities of provisions spoiled during the crossing.

35. Symmes, *History of the Old Tennent Church*, 106.

CHAPTER V: APPEAL TO A "CANDID WORLD"

1. *Lee Papers*, II, 435-436.

2. *Ibid.*, II, 437.

3. *Ibid.*, III, 206.

4. *Ibid.*, II, 437.

5. *Ibid.*, II, 438.

6. *Ibid.*, II, 440.

7. Fitzpatrick, *Writings of Washington*, XII, 142-143.

8. *Lee Papers*, III, 2.

9. *Ibid.*, II, 457-459.

10. *Ibid.*, II, 452-453.

11. *Ibid.*, II, 454, 456.

12. Thomas Gordon, *Gazatteer of the State of New Jersey*, 275.

13. *Lee Papers*, II, 438-440.

14. *Ibid.*, II, 467.

15. "Hamilton's Eulogium on Gen. Greene, July 4, 1789," *Magazine of American History*, III, 265.

16. Fisher, *The Struggle for American Independence*, II, 193.

17. *Lee Papers*, II, 450, 472-473.

18. William Watson to Joseph Lyman, July 4, 1778, Morristown National Historical Park Library, MSS # 650, Morristown, New Jersey.

19. Patterson, *Knight Errant of Liberty*, 207; Custis, *Recollections*, 290-291; Dr. Griffith to his wife, June 30, 1778, Manuscript Division, NYPL. Custis heard this story through Colonel George Nicolas.

20. Wharton, *Diplomatic Correspondence*, I, 280; Stryker, *Battle of Monmouth*, 171-172; Clinton, *American Rebellion*, 96n.

21. Clinton, *American Rebellion*, 91.

22. *Lee Papers*, III, 2-5, 8.

23. *Ibid.,* III, 7-8.

24. *Ibid.,* III, 149-150, 156.

25. *Ibid.,* III, 157-158.

26. *Ibid.,* III, 240-241; Stillé, *Wayne,* 145.

27. *Ibid.,* III, 208.

28. *Ibid.,* II, 458.

29. *Ibid.,* IV, 35.

30. *Ibid.,* II, 479-480.

31. *Ibid.,* III, 229.

32. *Ibid.,* III, 230-232, 272, 303-304, IV, 11.

33. *Ibid.,* III, 230-231.

34. *Ibid.,* III, 304.

35. Burnett, *Letters,* III, 465.

36. *Lee Papers,* III, 261.

37. *Journals of the Continental Congress,* XII, 1184, 1195; Alden, *Charles Lee,* 250-253.

38. *Ibid.*

39. *Lee Papers,* III, 237, 290, 304.

40. Alden, *Charles Lee,* 258.

41. *Lee Papers,* III, 463.

42. *Pennsylvania Magazine of History and Biography,* XXIX, 20.

43. Thacher, *Military Journal,* 176.

44. Lee, *Memoirs of the War in the Southern Department,* I, 63.

45. Alden, *Charles Lee,* 262ff.

46. Graydon, *Memoirs,* 323.

47. *Lee Papers,* III, 283-285; Steiner, *James McHenry,* 20n.

48. *Ibid.,* III, 283-285; Fisher, *The Struggle for American Independence,* II, 172; Graydon, 323, 341.

49. Alden, *Charles Lee,* 260-262.

50. *Lee Papers,* III, 305, 307-308, 317, 320, IV, 152-153, 321.

51. *Lee Papers,* III, 379.

52. *Ibid.,* III, 405-408.

53. *Ibid.,* IV, 3.

54. *Ibid.,* IV, 31.

55. *Ibid.,* IV, 31-32.

56. *Ibid.,* IV, 30-31.

57. Alden, *Charles Lee,* 298-299; Patterson, *Knight Errant of Liberty,* 278.

58. *Lee Papers,* IV, 37.

CHAPTER VI: IN THE EYES OF HISTORIANS

1. Gordon, *History of the Rise, Progress, and Establishment of the Independence of the United States,* II, 365-366.

2. Ramsay, *History of the American Revolution,* II, 85-86.

3. *Lee Papers,* IV, 125.

4. Stedman, *History of the Origins, Progress and Termination of the American War,* II, 21-24.

5. Weems, *Life of Washington,* 166-167.

6. Marshall, *Life of Washington,* III, 509, 517-520.

7. Holmes, *American Annals,* II, 283-284.

8. Lee, *Memoirs of the War in the Southern Department of the United States,* I, 59-60.

9. Allen, *A History of the American Revolution,* 184.

10. Johnson, *Nathanael Greene,* I, 104.

11. Hinton, *The History and Topography of the United States,* I, 271-272; Thomas Gordon, *Gazetteer of the State of New Jersey,* 273-275; Waln, *Life of the Marquis de La Fayette,* 89; Headley, *Washington and His Generals,* 157; Irving, *Life of Washington,* III, 433.

12. Thacher, *Military Journal,* 166; Graydon, *Memoirs,* 321-322.

13. Sparks, *Life of Washington,* 275.

14. Sparks, *Life of Charles Lee; Lee Papers,* IV, 312 ff.

15. Moore, *The Treason of Charles Lee,* vii ff.

16. Custis, *Recollections,* 219, 293n.

17. Schroeder and Lossing, *Life and Times of Washington,* III, 1197.

18. Lossing, *Life of Washington,* 623-632.

19. Bancroft, *History of the United States,* V, 274-275.

20. Fiske, *The American Revolution,* 75-80.

21. Tower, *La Fayette,* 348-357.

22. Wilson, *George Washington,* 202.

23. Tyler, *The Literary History of the American Revolution,* I, 400.

24. Carrington, *Battles of the American Revolution,* 419.

25. Stryker, *Battle of Monmouth,* 167; Stryker, "Lee's Conduct at the Battle of Monmouth," *Proceedings of the New Jersey Historical Society,* Third Series, II (1897), No. 2, 96-99.

26. Sargent, *Major John André,* 208-209.

27. Fisher, *The Struggle for American Independence,* II, 184-193.

28. Francis Vinton Greene, *The Revolutionary War,* 144-145.

29. Whipple, *The Story of Washington,* II, 50-63.

30. Channing, *A History of the United States,* III, 297.

31. Van Tyne, *The American Revolution,* 245.

32. Van Doren, *Secret History of the American Revolution,* 35.

33. Ward, *The War of the Revolution,* II, 580-582.

34. Miller, *Triumph of Freedom,* 325-326.

35. Stephenson and Dunn, *George Washington,* II, 90.

36. Lancaster, *From Lexington to Freedom,* 349-352.

37. Downey, "The Girls Behind the Guns," *American Heritage,* Vol. VIII, No. 1 (Dec., 1956), 48.

38. Callahan, *Henry Knox,* 144, 147.

39. Freeman, *George Washington,* V, 35, 43, 58.

40. Broadus Mitchell, *Alexander Hamilton,* I, 167-170.

41. Dupuy and Dupuy, *The Compact History of the Revolutionary War,* 284.

42. Morison, *Oxford History of the American People,* 250.

43. Bill, *New Jersey and the Revolutionary War,* 82.

44. Joseph B. Mitchell, *Discipline and Bayonets,* 109-111.

45. Flexner, *George Washington,* 314-315.

46. Woodward, *George Washington,* 352-357.

47. Preston, *Anthony Wayne,* 148.

48. Alden, *Charles Lee,* 175, 226-234, 245-279 (New York, 1969)

49. Alden, *The American Revolution,* 393.

50. Willcox, *Portrait of a General,* 234-235.

51. Shy, "Charles Lee," *George Washington's Generals,* 45.

52. Patterson, *Knight Errant of Liberty,* 280.

53. Wandell and Minnigerode, *Aaron Burr,* I, 60; Greene, *Nathanael Greene,* II, 94.

Bibliography

Adams, Charles Francis, ed. *The Works of John Adams.* 10 vols. Boston, 1850–1856.

——. *Familiar Letters of John Adams and His Wife, Abigail Adams.* New York, 1876.

Alden, John Richard. *The American Revolution.* New York, 1969.

——. *General Charles Lee: Traitor or Patriot?* Baton Rouge, La., 1951.

Allen, Paul. *A History of the American Revolution.* 2 vols. Baltimore, 1822.

Anderson, Troyer S. *The Command of the Howe Brothers.* New York, 1936.

André, John. *Major André's Journal.* Tarrytown, N. Y., 1930.

Annual Register or a View of the History, Politics, and Literature for the Year 1778. London, 1796,

Bancroft, George. *History of the United States of America.* 6 vols. Boston, 1886. (Reprinted Kennikat Press, Port Washington, N.Y.).

Bass, Robert D. *The Green Dragoon: The Lives of Banastre Tarleton and Mary Robinson.* New York, 1957.

Baurmeister, Major. "Letters from Major Baurmeister to Colonel von Jungkenn written during the Philadelphia Campaign, 1777-1778," *Pennsylvania Magazine of History and Biography,* LX (1936).

——. *Revolution in America: Baurmeister Journals,* ed. B.A. Uhlendorf and Edna Vosper. New Brunswick, N.J., 1957.

Belcher, Henry. *The First American Civil War.* London, 1911.

Bill, Alfred H. *New Jersey and the Revolutionary War.* New York, 1964.

Boudinot, Elias. *Journal or Historical Recollections of American Events During the Revolutionary War.* Philadelphia, 1894.

Burnett, Edmund C. *Letters of Members of the Continental Congress.* 8 vols. Washington, 1921-1936.

Burr, Aaron. *Memoirs of Aaron Burr,* ed. Matthew L. Davis. 2 vols. New York, 1836-1837.

Callahan, North. *Daniel Morgan: Ranger of the Revolution.* New York, 1961.

——. *Henry Knox: General Washington's General.* New York, 1958.

Carrington, Henry B. *Battles of the American Revolution.* New York, 1876.

Channing, Edward. *A History of the United States.* 6 vols. New York, 1905-1925.

Chitwood, Oliver P. *Richard Henry Lee: Statesman of the Revolution.* Morgantown, W. Va., 1967.

Clinton, George. *The Public Papers of George Clinton.* New York, 1899-1914.

Clinton, Henry. *The American Rebellion,* ed. William B. Willcox, New Haven, 1954.

Coffin, Charles. *The Lives and Services of Major General John Thomas, Col. Thomas Knowlton, Col. Alexander Scammell, and Major General Henry Dearborn.* New York, 1845.

Cook, Fred J. *What Manner of Men: Forgotten Heroes of the American Revolution.* New York, 1960.

Custis, George Washington. *Recollections and Private Memoirs of Washington.* New York, 1860.

Dearborn, Henry. *Journal, 1776-1783.* Cambridge, Mass., 1887.

Dictionary of American Biography, ed. Allen Johnson. 2 vols. New York, 1957.

Donehoo, George P. *Pennsylvania, A History.* New York, 1926.

Downey, Fairfax D. "The Girls Behind the Guns," *American Heritage* Vol. VIII, No. 1, (Dec., 1956).

Doyle, Joseph B. *Frederick William Von Steuben and the American Revolution.* Steubenville, Ohio, 1913.

Dupuy, Ernest and Trevor. *The Compact History of the Revolutionary War.* New York, 1963.

Eelking, Max von. *The German Allied Troops in the North American War of Independence 1776-1783.* Albany, 1893.

Ellet, Elizabeth F. *Domestic History of the American Revolution.* New York, 1850.

——. *The Women of the American Revolution.* 3 vols. New York, 1848-1850.

Ellis, Franklin. *A History of Monmouth County, New Jersey.* Philadelphia, 1885.

Fisher, Sydney George. *The Struggle for American Independence.* 2 vols. Philadelphia, 1908.

Fiske, John. *The American Revolution.* 2 vols. New York, 1891.

Fitzpatrick, John C., ed. *The Writings of George Washington.* 39 vols. Washington, 1931-1938.

Flexner, James T. *George Washington in the American Revolution, 1775-1783.* Boston, 1968.

Freeman, Douglas S. *George Washington, a Biography.* 5 vols. New York, 1948-1952.

Frost, John. *The Battle Grounds of America.* Auburn, N.Y., 1846.

Gordon, Thomas F. *A Gazetteer of the State of New Jersey.* Trenton, 1834.

Gordon, William. *History of the Rise, Progress, and Establishment of the Independence of the United States of America.* 4 vols. London, 1788; New York, 1801.

Gottschalk, Louis. *Lafayette Joins the American Army.* Chicago, 1937.

Graham, Joseph. *Life of General Daniel Morgan.* New York, 1856.

Graydon, Alexander. *Memoirs of His Own Times.* Philadelphia, 1846.

BIBLIOGRAPHY

Greene, Francis V. *The Revolutionary War.* New York, 1911. (Reprinted Kennikat Press, Port Washington, N.Y.).

Greene, George Washington. *Life of Nathanael Greene.* 3 vols. New York, 1867-1871.

Griffin, Martin L. *Stephen Moylan.* Philadelphia, 1909.

Headley, Joel T. *Washington and His Generals.* New York, 1847.

Higginbotham, Don. *Daniel Morgan: Revolutionary Rifleman.* Chapel Hill, N.C., 1961.

Hillard, Elias B. *The Last Men of the Revolution.* Hartford, Conn., 1864.

Hinton, John H., ed., *The History and Topography of the United States.* Philadelphia, 1830-1832.

Holmes, Abiel. *American Annals.* Cambridge, Mass., 1805.

Ingles, Charles James. *The Queen's Rangers in the Revolutionary War.* Aylmer East, Canada, 1956.

Irving, Washington. *Life of George Washington.* 5 vols. New York, 1860.

Jefferson, Thomas. *The Papers of Thomas Jefferson,* ed. Julian Boyd. Vols. 4-6, Princeton, 1951-1952.

Johnson, William. *Sketches of the Life and Correspondence of Nathanael Greene.* 2 vols. Charleston, S.C., 1822.

Johnston, Henry B. "The Campaign of 1776 around New York and Brooklyn," *Memoirs of the Long Island Historical Society,* Vol. III. Brooklyn, 1878.

Jones, Thomas P. *History of New York during the Revolutionary War.* 2 vols. New York, 1879.

Journal of American History. 29 vols. New Haven, 1907-1935.

Journals of the Continental Congress, 1774-1789, ed. Worthington C. Ford and Gaillard Hunt. 34 vols. Washington, 1904-1937.

Kapp, Friedrich. *The Life of Frederick William Von Steuben.* New York, 1859.

Kirkland, Frederic R. *Letters on the American Revolution at the Library at Karolfred.* Philadelphia, 1941.

Kite, Elizabeth S. *Brigadier General Louis Lebeque Duportail.* Baltimore, 1933.

Knollenberg, Bernard. *Washington and the Revolution.* New York, 1941.

Lafayette, Marquis de. *Letters to Washington,* ed. Louis Gottschalk. New York, 1944.

——. *Memoirs, Correspondence and Manuscripts of General Lafayette.* 3 vols. London, 1837.

Lancaster, Bruce. *From Lexington to Liberty.* New York, 1955.

Langworthy, Edward. *Memoirs of the Life of the Late Charles Lee.* New York, 1792.

Laurens, John. *The Army Correspondence of Colonel John Laurens,* ed. William Gilmore Simms. New York, 1867.

Lee, Charles. *Lee Papers, New-York Historical Society Collections.* 4 vols. New York, 1871-1874.

Lee, Henry. *Memoirs of the War in the Southern Department of the United States.* 2 vols. Philadelphia, 1812.

Lee, Richard Henry. *Memoirs of the Life of Richard Henry Lee and His Correspondence with the Most Distinguished Men in America and Europe.* 2 Vols. Philadelphia, 1825.

Lodge, H.C., ed. *The Works of Alexander Hamilton.* 12 vols. New York, 1904.

BIBLIOGRAPHY

Lossing, Benson J. *The Pictorial Field Book of the Revolution.* 2 vols. New York, 1851-1852.

——. *Life of Washington.* New York, 1860.

Lovell, Louise L. *Israel Angell, Colonel of the 2nd. Rhode Island Regiment.* New York, 1921.

Lowell, Edward J. *The Hessians in the Revolution.* New York, 1884.

Lundin, Leonard. *Cockpit of the American Revolution: The War for Independence in New Jersey,* Princeton, 1940.

Magazine of American History, with Notes and Queries. 30 vols. New York, 1877-1893.

Marshall, John. *Life of George Washington.* 5 vols. Philadelphia, 1804-1807.

Martin, James Sullivan. *A Narrative of Some of the Adventures, Dangers and Sufferings of a Revolutionary Soldier,* ed. Joseph P. Martin. Hallowell, Maine, 1830. Published also as *Private Yankee Doodle.* Boston, 1962.

Miller, John C. *Triumph of Freedom, 1775-1783.* Boston, 1948.

Mitchell, Broadus. *Alexander Hamilton, Youth to Maturity, 1755-1788.* New York, 1957.

Mitchell, Joseph B. *Discipline and Bayonets.* New York, 1967.

Montresor, John. "Journals of Capt. John Montresor," *New-York Historical Society Collections* (1875). New York, 1876.

Montross, Lynn. *Rag, Tag and Bobtail: The Story of the Continental Army.* New York, 1952.

Moore, Frank. *Diary of the American Revolution from Newspapers and Original Documents.* 2 vols. New York, 1860.

Moore, George H. *The Treason of Charles Lee.* New York, 1860. (Reprinted by Kennikat Press, Port Washington, N.Y.).

Morison, Samuel Eliot. *Oxford History of the American People.* New York, 1965.

Morris, Richard B. *Alexander Hamilton and the Founding of the Nation.* New York, 1957.

New Jersey Archives. Documents Relating to the Colonial, Revolutionary, and Post-revolutionary History of the State of New Jersey, 41 vols. Newark, 1880-1949.

New Jersey. Minutes of the Governor's Privy Council, 1777-1796, I. State Library, Trenton.

Orderly Book of the Maryland Loyalist Regiment, ed. P.L. Ford. Brooklyn, 1891.

Palmer, John M. *General Von Steuben.* New Haven, 1937. (Reprinted by Kennikat Press, Port Washington, N.Y.).

Parton, James. *The Life and Times of Aaron Burr.* New York, 1858.

Patterson, Samuel W. *Knight Errant of Liberty: The Triumph and Tragedy of General Charles Lee.* New York, 1958.

Pennsylvania Magazine of History and Biography, XIV (1890), "Notes on the Battle of Monmouth," reprinted from the London Chronicle of Sept. 19-22, 1778.

Preston, John H. *A Gentleman Rebel: The Exploits of Anthony Wayne.* New York, 1930.

Ramsay, David. *History of the American Revolution.* 2 vols. Philadelphia, 1789.

BIBLIOGRAPHY

Read, D.B. *The Life and Times of General John Graves Sincoe.* Toronto, 1890.

Reed, William B. *Life and Correspondence of Joseph Reed.* 2 vols. Philadelphia, 1847.

Salter, Edwin. *A History of Monmouth and Ocean Counties.* Bayonne, N.J., 1890.

Salter, Edwin and George C. Beekman. *Old Times in Old Monmouth.* Freehold, N.J., 1887.

Sargent, Winthrop. *The Life and Career of Major John André.* New York, 1902.

Scales, John. *Life of General Joseph Cilly.* Manchester, N.H., 1921.

Scheer, George F., and Hugh F. Rankin. *Rebels and Redcoats.* New York, 1957.

Serle, Ambrose. *The American Journal of Ambrose Serle, Secretary to Lord Howe, 1776-1778,* ed. Edward Tatum. San Marino, Calif., 1940.

Shaw, Samuel. *Journals.* Boston, 1847.

Schroeder, John F., and Benson J. Lossing. *Life and Times of Washington.* New York, 1878.

Shy, John. "Charles Lee," *George Washington's Generals.* New York, 1964.

Simcoe, John Graves. *Military Journal.* New York, 1844.

Smith, Samuel S. *The Battle of Monmouth.* Monmouth Beach, N.J., 1964.

Sparks, Jared. *Correspondence of the American Revolution being Letters of Eminent Men to George Washington.* 4 vols. Boston, 1853.

——. *The Life of George Washington.* Boston, 1839.

——. *Life of Charles Lee, Major General in the Army of the Revolution.* Boston, 1846.

Stedman, Charles. *History of the Origins, Progress and Termination of the American War.* 2 vols. London, 1794.

Steiner, B.C. *Life and Correspondence of James McHenry.* Cleveland, 1907.

Stephenson, Nathaniel W. and Waldo H. Dunn. *George Washington.* New York, 1940.

Stillé, Charles J. *Major-General Anthony Wayne and the Pennsylvania Line of the Continental Army.* Philadelphia, 1893. (Reprinted by Kennikat Press, Port Washington, N.Y.).

Stryker, William S. *Battle of Monmouth.* Princeton, 1927. (Reprinted by Kennikat Press, Port Washington, N.Y.).

Stuart, Sir Charles. *New Records of the American Revolution; Letters, Manuscripts and Documents sent by Sir Charles Stuart, to his Father, the Earl of Bute, 1775-1779.* Privately Printed 193-

Symmes, Frank R. *History of the Old Tennent Church.* Freehold, N.J., 1897.

Syrett, Harold C., ed. *Hamilton Papers.* 11 vols., New York, 1961-1969.

Thacher, James. *Military Journal during the American Revolutionary War.* Boston, 1833.

Thayer, Theodore. *Nathanael Greene: Strategist of the American Revolution.* New York, 1960.

Tower, Charlemagne. *The Marquis De La Fayette in the American Revolution.* 2 vols. Philadelphia, 1895.

Townsend, Sara B. *An American Soldier: The Life of John Laurens.* Raleigh, N.C., 1958.

Tyler, Moses C. *The Literary History of the American Revolution, 1763-1783.* 2 vols. New York, 1897.

BIBLIOGRAPHY

Van Doren, Carl. *Secret History of the American Revolution.* New York, 1941.

Van Tyne, Claude. *The American Revolution* (American Nation Series, v.9). New York, 1905.

Waln, Robert. *Life of the Marquis de la Fayette.* Philadelphia, 1825.

Wandell, Samuel H., and Meade Minnigerode. *Aaron Burr.* New York, 1927.

Ward, Christopher. *The War of the Revolution.* 2 vols. New York, 1952.

——. *The Delaware Continentals, 1776-1783.* Wilmington, 1941.

Watson, John F. *Annals of Philadelphia.* Philadelphia, 1898.

Weems, Mason L. *A History of the Life and Death, Virtues and Exploits of General George Washington.* Philadelphia, 1800.

Wharton, Francis, ed. *The Revolutionary Diplomatic Correspondence of the United States.* 6 vols. Washington, 1889.

Whipple, Wayne. *The Story-Life of Washington.* Philadelphia, 1911.

Wickwire, Franklin and Mary. *Cornwallis: The American Adventure.* Boston, 1970.

Willcox, William B. *Portrait of a General: Sir Henry Clinton in the War of Independence.* New York, 1964.

——. "British Strategy in America, 1778," *Journal of Modern History* (June, 1947.

Williams, Catherine R. *Biography of Revolutionary Heroes.* Providence, 1839.

Wilson, Woodrow, *George Washington.* New York, 1896.

Woodward, E.E. *George Washington: The Image and the Man.* New York, 1926.

Index

INDEX

Map No. 3

Lee Defends at Bridge While Washington Forms Main Army

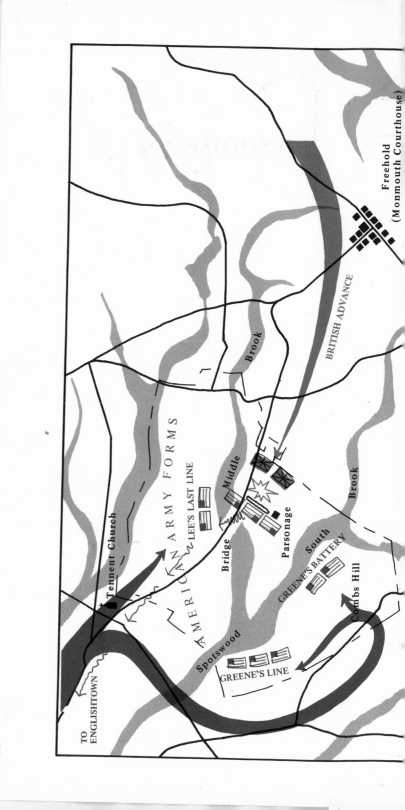